NAVAJO RUGS AND BLANKETS
A Coloring Book

By Chuck and Andrea Mobley
Illustrated by Sam Mike

Treasure Chest Publications, Inc.
P.O. Box 5250
Tucson, Arizona 85703-0250

ISBN 0-918080-76-2

Copyright © 1994 by Chuck and Andrea Mobley

Printed in the USA
Printing 10 9 8 7 6 5 4 3 2 1

This book is dedicated to
The weavers for their spirit,
The people of Greasewood and Ganado for their
friendship,
And to Ed Chamberlin for his inspiration

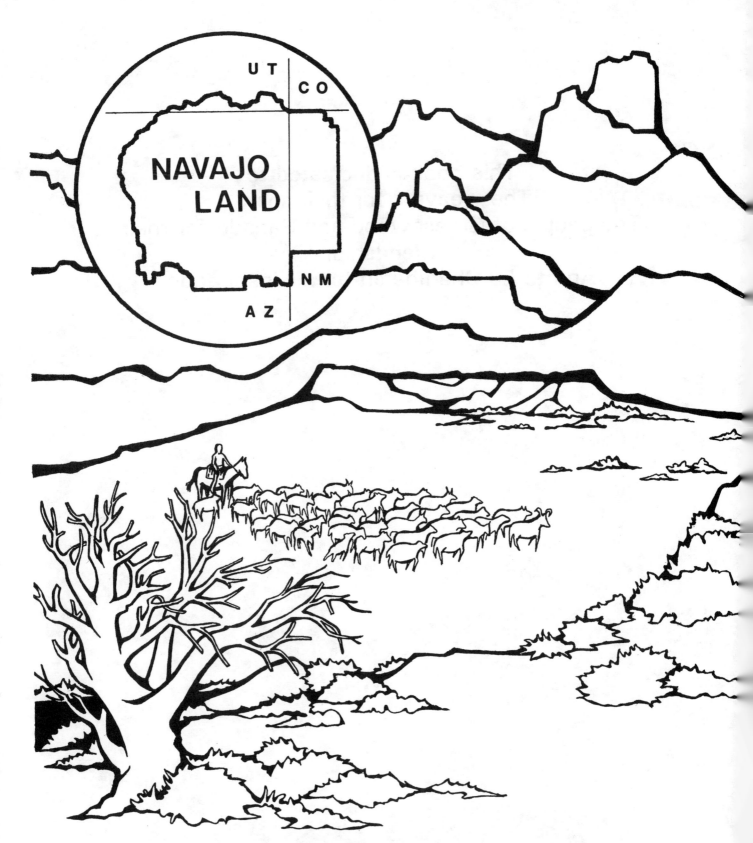

The Navajo Indian Reservation is in parts of Arizona, New Mexico, and Utah. The Navajo, or Dineh as they call themselves, have lived there for over 500 years.

Many Navajo live in round houses called hogans. At one time hogans were made out of earth and logs. Modern hogans are made mostly of wood.

The Navajo have a long history with many traditions. They are famous for many arts and crafts, but they are most famous for their weaving.

The Navajo learned to weave from the Pueblo Indians who lived close by. The Navajo soon became very good weavers.

At first the Navajo used the weavings for blankets, rugs, and clothing.

When trading posts opened in the early 1800's, the Navajo began to trade their rugs for food and other things they needed.

The traders sold the rugs and blankets to other people. The traders helped the Navajo weavers by telling them what colors and designs the people liked.

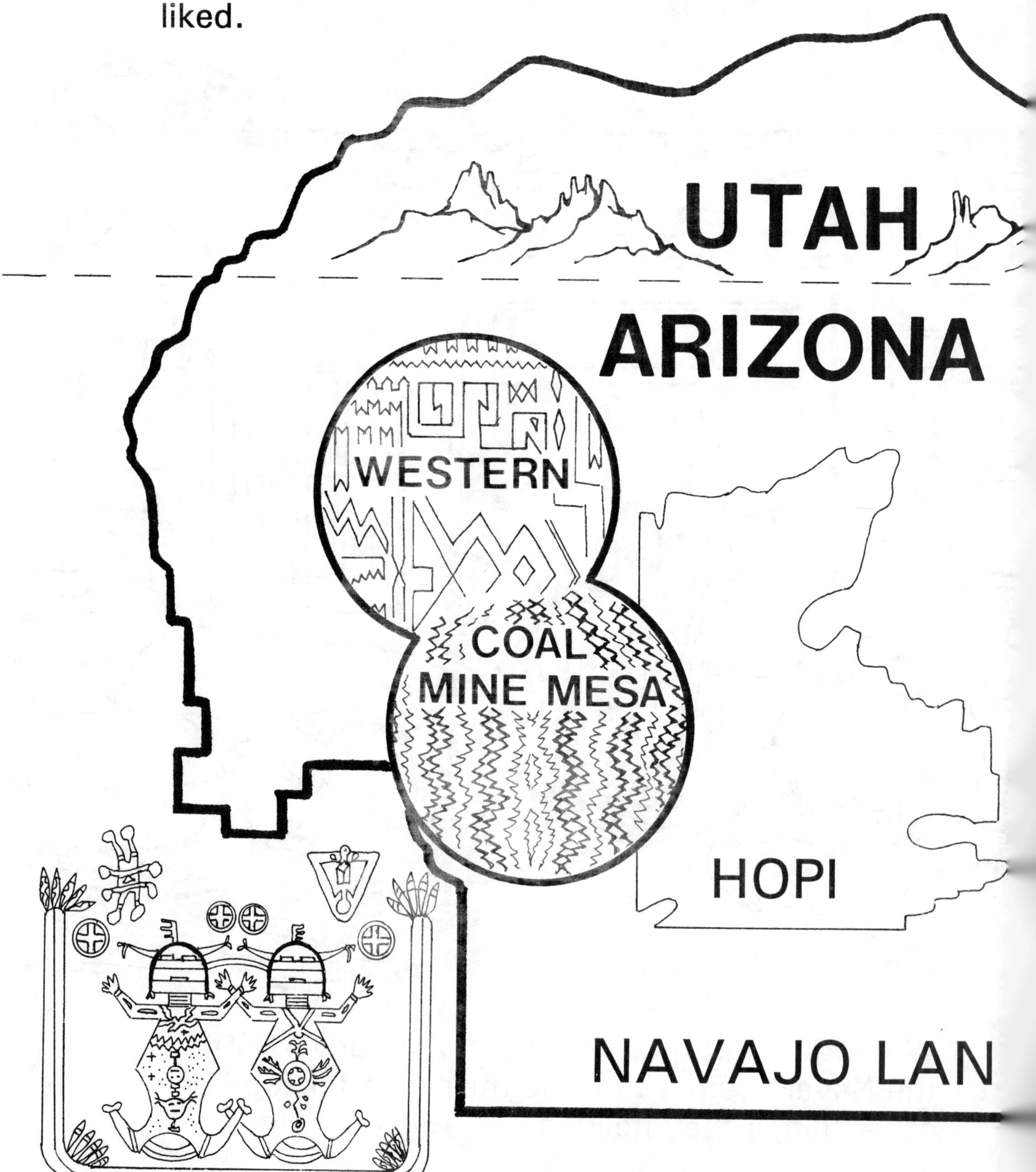

UTAH

ARIZONA

WESTERN

COAL MINE MESA

HOPI

NAVAJO LAN

There are many different kinds of Navajo rugs.
They are named for the area of the reservation
where they were first made.

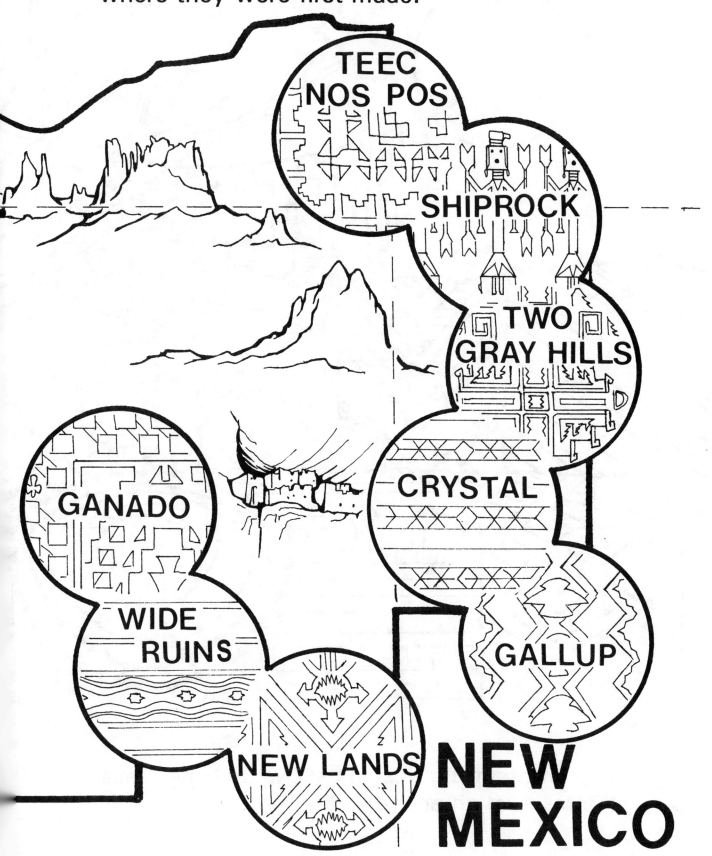

The different rug designs show that the areas of the reservation are very different.

The rugs are made out of wool. Wool comes from sheep. Many Navajo still raise their own sheep. Others buy the wool from stores.

Parts of plants are used to dye, or color the wool.

SUMAC BARK
dark brown

(red)
ONION SKINS (brown)
medium brown — orange

JUNIPER ROOT
medium brown

SUMAC BERRIES
light brown

ROSE HIPS
red brown

The wool is trimmed, or sheared from the sheep.

PIÑON PITCH
black

BLACK WALNUT SHELLS
black

WILD BLACK BERRIES
grey

GOLDEN ROD
yellow

Then it is carded, or brushed to clean and strengthen it.

Next, the wool is twisted (spun) into yarn that is strong and hard to break.

The Navajo use a loom to hold the wool in place as they weave. It has strings going up and down. They pull the yarn in and out across the strings. It is very hard work and takes a long time to weave a rug.

Color with red, grey, black, and white

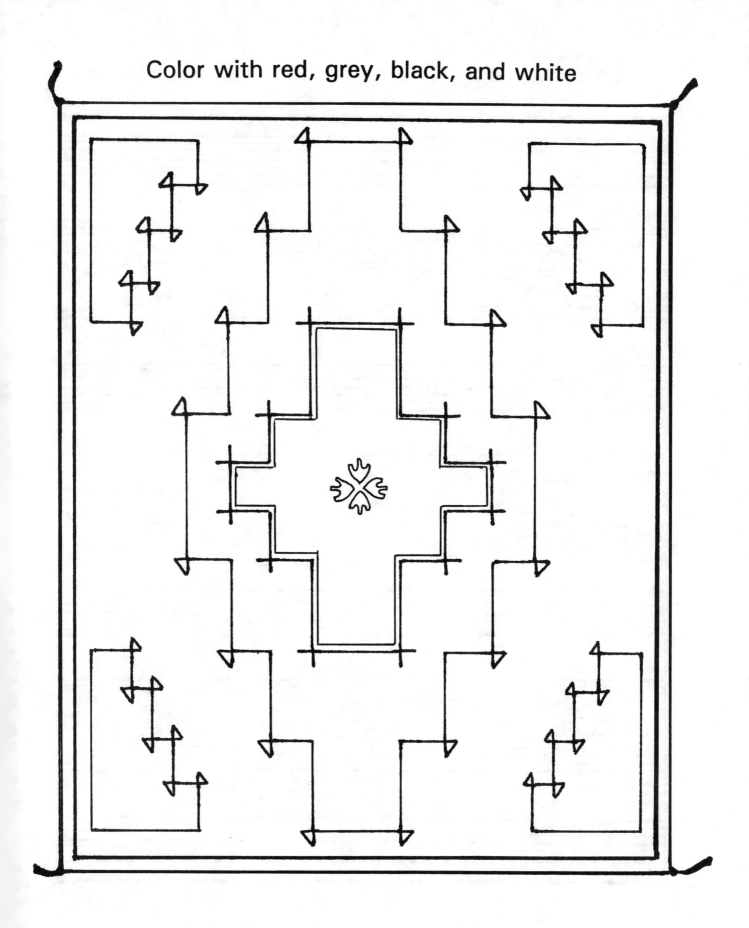

Ganado (ga na' doe) Red design from Ganado, Arizona

Color with light colors of pink, blue, and yellow

Wide Ruins design from Wide Ruins, Arizona

Color any color you wish

Chinle (chin' lee) design from Chinle, Arizona

Color with bright colors of red, orange, and green

Teec Nos Pos (Teese' nos paws) design from
Teec Nos Pos, Arizona

Color red, grey, black, and any color

Storm Pattern design from Tonalea, Arizona

Color background grey or brown
The rest may be any bright color

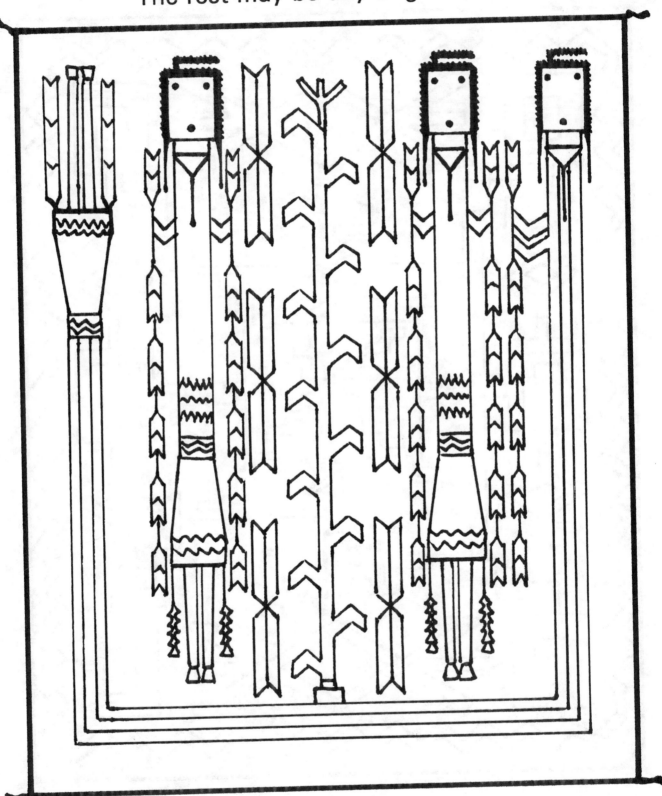

A Yei (yea) design from Shiprock, New Mexico

Colors are always grey, brown, black, and white

Two Grey Hills design from Two Grey Hills,
New Mexico

Color any color you wish

Gallup Throw Rug design from Gallup, New Mexico

Color any color you wish

Crystal design from Crystal, New Mexico

Color any color you wish

Eye Dazzler design from all areas of reservation

Color blue, red, black, and white

Chief Blanket design from all areas of reservation

Color red, grey, black, and white

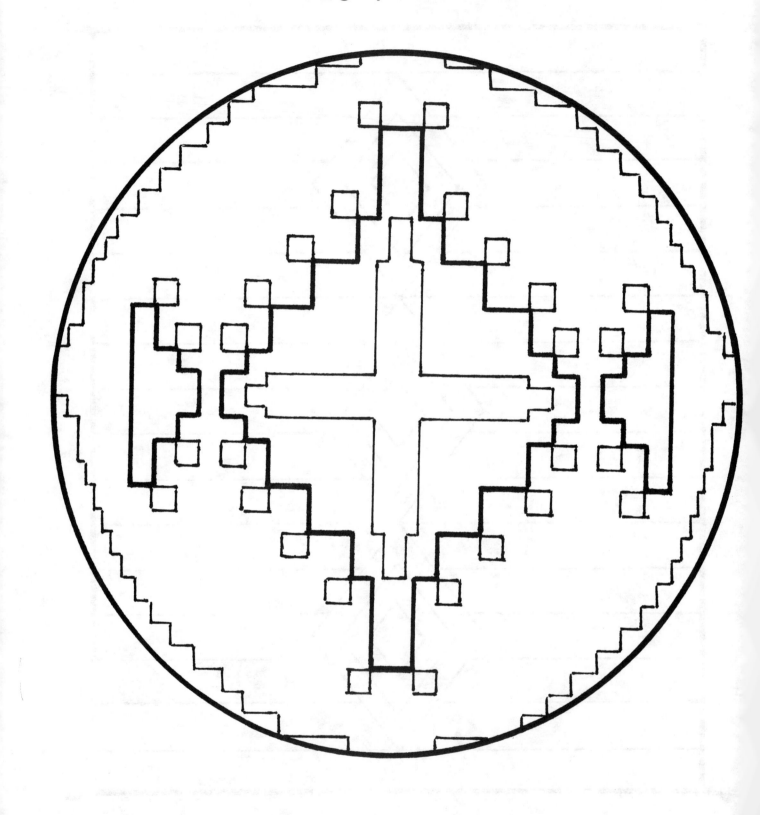

Round rug design from Ganado, Arizona

Color red, grey, black, and white

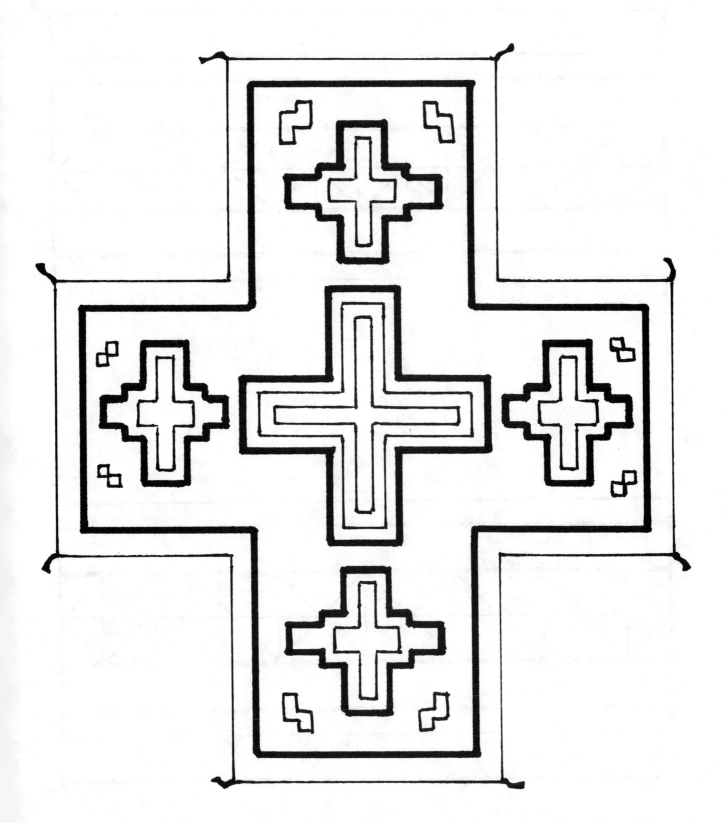

Cross design from Ganado, Arizona

Color red, black or blue

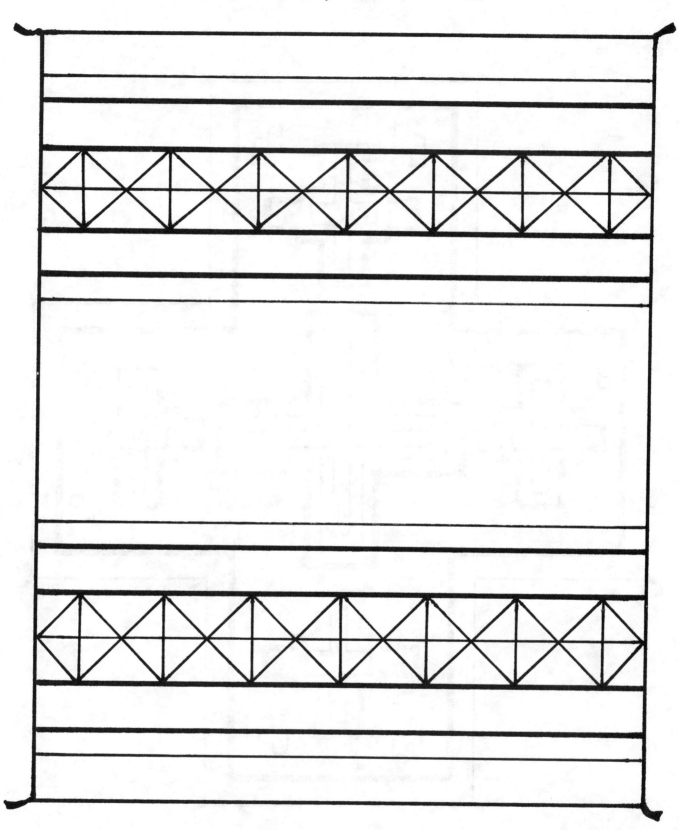

Woman's dress from all areas of the reservation

Color any color you wish

Design your own Navajo rug

Color any color you wish

Design your own Navajo rug

FIFTY-FIFTY

A speaking and listening course

BOOK ONE

Third Edition

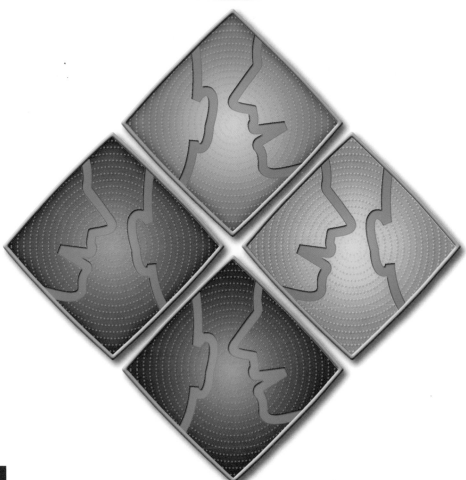

PEARSON
Longman

WARREN WILSON • ROGER BARNARD

Published by
Pearson Longman Asia ELT
20/F Cornwall House
Taikoo Place
979 King's Road
Quarry Bay
Hong Kong

fax: +852 2856 9578
email: pearsonlongman.hk@pearson.com
www.pearsonlongman.com

and Associated Companies throughout the world.

First edition 1992
Second edition 1998
This edition 2007
Reprinted 2013

Produced by Pearson Education Asia Limited, Hong Kong
GCC/26

ISBN-13: 978-962-00-5665-9

Publisher: Rachel Wilson
Editor: Richard Whitbread
Designers: Junko Funaki, Jack Wong
Illustrators: Roger Barnard, Megan Cash, Andrew Lange, Teddy Wong

Acknowledgments

We would like to thank the following reviewers for the insightful feedback
provided for this edition: Yu-Ping Chang, Pei-Ling (Bessie) Chuang, Patrick
Davis, John Doodigian, William Figoni, Daniel Gossman, Jennifer Hickey,
Christopher Kerr, Kitai Kim, Carmella Lieske, Moon-Jeong Lim, John
Matthews, Michael S. Neiburg, Hugh Palmer, Trafford Parry, Caleb Prichard,
Andrew Reinmann, Richard H. Schaepe, Mike Shearer, Kenji Takahashi,
Marissa Troxell and David Whitmore.

CONTENTS

Acknowledgments

We would like to thank the teachers and students at the following schools for their valuable help in developing and revising this material:

- Athénée-Français, Tokyo
- Community English Program, Teachers College, Columbia University, New York
- Cosmopolitan Language Institute, Tokyo
- English Language Institute, Queens College, New York
- Haggerty English Language Program, SUNY New Paltz, New York
- International English Language Institute, Hunter College, New York
- Tama Art University, Tokyo
- Tokyo School of Business, Tokyo

We would also like to thank those at Prentice Hall who worked on this project originally, particularly our first production editor, Noël Vreeland Carter. For this new edition, we owe much to our publisher, Rachel Wilson, our editor, Richard Whitbread, our design manager, Winnie Sung, and her team of talented designers including Junko Funaki, Tonic Ng and Jack Wong, and all the great people at Pearson Longman.

For Masako, Sophie, In Sook, Mia and Dale.

R.B.
W.W.
Tokyo / New York
September 2006

INTRODUCTION

Fifty-Fifty Third Edition is a three-level course in communicative English that provides listening and speaking practice for students from the elementary level through the intermediate level. Designed primarily for use in large classes where "student talking" time is usually very limited, this material can be used effectively in virtually any size class since students actively participate in meaningful exchanges during pair work and group work. The focus is on listening and speaking proficiency. *Fifty-Fifty* Third Edition provides realistic yet manageable listening tasks, and extended pair work and group work tasks, all of which are designed to reduce learner anxiety and promote language acquisition via student participation in purposeful interaction.

Fifty-Fifty Book One has been designed as a follow-up course to *Fifty-Fifty Intro*, and can be used in classes at the high-elementary/low-intermediate level. The text consists of a warm-up unit, twelve main units and three review units. The *Appendix* contains the *Student B pages* of the pair work and group work activities, the *Self-study exercises* with *Answer key* for out-of-class review and the *Audio script* for the *Listening tasks*.

Each unit consists of the following sections. (The format of the review units differs slightly.)

● Warm-up exercises

Each unit begins with some simple warm-up exercises. *Exercise 1* is in the form of a comic sketch. The sketch has a question or an answer to be written by the student. The sketch illustrates the unit theme and introduces, in a simple context, the language to be practiced.

Exercise 2 and *Exercise 3* center on a dialogue that functions as a model that the students can listen to and practice reading through with a partner. The dialogue can also be used for freer conversation practice in which the students supply their own information.

● Listening task

The *Listening task* helps the students focus on the particular language points to be practiced. The students are not expected to retain or reproduce *all* the language they hear on the recording, but their aural comprehension of the target structures and vocabulary will increase as they listen for the information needed to complete the task.

It is suggested that the students listen several times: once to familiarize the students with the content, then again with pauses as the students complete the task and once more straight through as they check their answers. After the teacher has elicited the answers, the students could listen a final time, perhaps while going over the audio script. The *Audio script* for the *Listening task* is located in the *Appendix* and can also be used for extended practice and/or review of grammar and vocabulary. The *Teacher's Edition* provides helpful hints, as well as the answers, to ensure that the exercise goes smoothly.

● Speaking task one

Speaking task one provides communicative practice that maximizes "student talking" time. Students complete the task by asking partners for missing information. Being task-based, the exercise provides more than just question-and-answer practice: genuine communication takes place. The completion of each task relies on actual information sharing and feedback between students conversing in pairs.

It is suggested that the teacher try having students sit face to face, if possible, and maintain eye contact while speaking. They should avoid looking at each other's pages and should always ask for spelling or repetition in English. It is advisable to circulate once quickly at the outset to make sure that each student understands what to do and gets off to a good start. Correction techniques vary from teacher to teacher and exercise to exercise; however, during communicative practice it is usually advisable to leave most correction until afterward. The point of the tasks is communication, not the production of flawless sentences. (Nevertheless, errors that interfere with comprehension and/or are counterproductive to the practice should be rectified appropriately.)

Finally, the teacher can check the finished work by scanning students' pages and briefly querying their partners to verify answers. Students can also confer and compare answers themselves.

● Speaking task two

Speaking task two is generally a bit "freer" than *Speaking task one* and is meant to provide additional practice in a slightly different context. *Speaking task two* exercises include "Find someone who" activities, group interviews and various types of language games that promote interaction while lessening learner anxiety.

All suggestions given above for *Speaking task one* apply to this section; the recommended procedures are the same.

● Language game

In the review units, *Speaking task two* is followed by a section labeled *Language game*, an activity that encourages focused listening. The point of the game is to provide ample comprehensible input containing vocabulary and structures from the preceding units, as well as pronunciation practice—hopefully more in an atmosphere of fun, and less of conscious language study.

● Homework

The last page of each main unit contains the *Homework* section, which is a brief writing assignment that students must do on a separate sheet of paper to be handed in. The *Homework* section includes a *Homework review* exercise, an optional follow-up exercise for in-class use, time permitting. Please note that some of these exercises might require the teacher's correction of the students' written homework before it is used as an oral/aural activity in class.

● Language focus

The *Language focus* section at the end of each main unit contains an overview of the sentence structures presented in the unit, providing language models for the students that they can use for a quick reference while doing the exercises.

● Student B pages

Student A, turn to page 3

This section in the *Appendix* contains all the pages necessary for the information gap activities, when students working in pairs or small groups must look at different pages. In the units, these activities contain a page reference in the upper right-hand corner. It might be a good idea to remind students not to look at their partner's pages or to flip back and forth between the *Student A* and *Student B pages*.

● Self-study exercises and Answer key

The *Self-study exercises* in the *Appendix* review and consolidate material covered in the twelve main units, providing students with added listening practice through recycling some of the *Listening task* audio. The accompanying *Answer key* provides all of the answers to the *Self-study exercises* and enables students to assess their own performance and their progress towards aural mastery of the listening material. Students can download the *Self-study Audio* by visiting the *Fifty-Fifty* website at www.fifty-fifty-series.com

● Audio script

The *Audio script* in the *Appendix* contains the *Listening task* material. The introductory dialogue in the *Warm-up exercises* of each unit is not included in the *Audio script* since the dialogue itself serves as the script.

In addition to the Student Book, the *Fifty-Fifty* series includes the following components:
- Teacher's Edition with Test Master CD-ROM Pack
- Class CD
- Companion Website: www.fifty-fifty-series.com
- Downloadable: Self-study Audio
- Downloadable: Class Audio

The authors hope you and your students enjoy using *Fifty-Fifty* Third Edition and would appreciate any comments or suggestions you might have. They can be contacted via the *Fifty-Fifty* website.

GETTING STARTED

Introductory exercises

Warm-up exercises

Look at page 4

Exercise 1

Write the man's question.

Exercise 3

Exercise 2 1

Listen to the following conversation. Then practice it with a partner.

Memo

Always look at the person you are speaking to. Don't look down at the page!

Teacher	Let's take turns. First, tell us your name and country.
Lina	I'll go first. My name's Lina, and I'm from Italy.
Teacher	Where do you live?
Lina	I live in Riverside.
Teacher	Do you have any hobbies?
Lina	Yes, I do. My hobbies are swimming and hiking.

Exercise 3

Practice the conversation a few more times. Each time, answer the questions with true information.

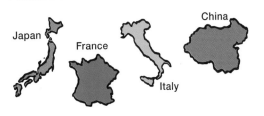

Look at page 4
Language focus

Listening task

Exercise 1 2–5

Listen to each person (1–4) and write the number next to the correct picture.

> **Memo**
>
> *Key sentences* are the important sentences that tell you which picture to choose.

Exercise 2 2–5

Listen again and write the *key sentence* below each picture.

Speaking task one

Listen to Student B and answer the questions. If you have blanks, ask Student B questions and fill in the blanks.

> **Memo**
>
> • For spelling ask, "How do you spell that?"
> • In box 4 you can use your hometown to answer the question "Where are you from?"

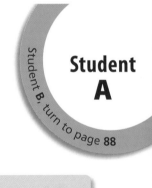

Student B, turn to page 88

Student A

1

| name |
| lives in |
| California <br> from |
| golf and swimming <br> hobbies |

2

| Tim and Liz <br> name |
| live in |
| England <br> from |
| hobbies |

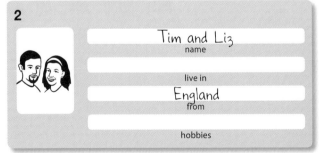

3
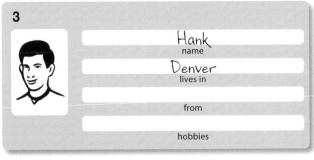

| Hank <br> name |
| Denver <br> lives in |
| from |
| hobbies |

4

| name |
| lives in |
| from |
| hobbies |

Student B

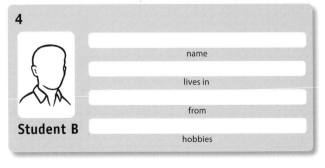

Speaking task two

Exercise 1

Write where your partner (from Speaking task one) lives and where your partner is from on the board.

Memo

Just write the places, not sentences.

Exercise 2 Do this exercise with everyone.

Walk around the classroom and talk to your classmates. Find out where four of your classmates live and where they are from, and fill in the boxes below. Ask yes/no questions using the places on the board.

Memo

Ask *only* yes/no questions!

Talk in *pairs*, not groups.

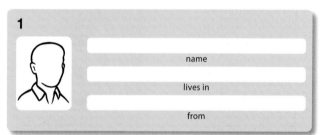

1

name

lives in

from

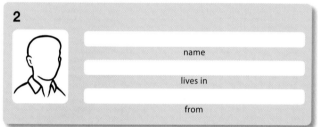

2

name

lives in

from

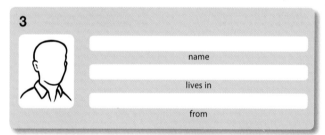

3

name

lives in

from

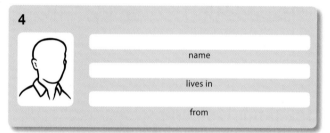

4

name

lives in

from

Language focus

| Where | do | you / they | live? | | I / We / They | live | in | New York. |
| | does | he / she | | | He / She | lives | | Boston. |

Where	are	you / they	from?		I'm		from	France.
	is	he / she			He's / She's			Hokkaido.
					We're / They're			Seoul.

Are	you / they	from	Busan?		Yes,	I	am.	No,	I'm	not.
Is	he / she					he / she	is.		he / she	isn't.
						we / they	are.		we / they	aren't.

| Do | you / they | have any hobbies? | | Yes, | I / we / they | do. | No, | I / we / they | don't. |
| Does | he / she | live in Tokyo? | | | he / she | does. | | he / she | doesn't. |

| My / Our / Their / His / Her | hobbies are hiking and playing tennis. |
| | hobby is rock climbing. |

Warm-up exercises

Exercise 1

Write the woman's question.

Exercise 2 6

Listen to the following conversation. Then practice it with a partner.

Memo

Always look at the person you are speaking to. Don't look down at the page!

Bernice	Oh, hi. Are you the new guy?
Andrew	Yes, I am. I started yesterday.
Bernice	Do you know how to use the cash register?
Andrew	No, I don't. Sorry.
Bernice	That's OK. I can show you. So, can you ski?
Andrew	Yes I can, but only a little.

Exercise 3

Practice the conversation a few more times. Each time, use the ideas below or your own ideas.

Look at page 10

Language focus

Listening task

Exercise 1 7

Listen to the conversation and check (✓) the things each person can do.

Dick										
Dad										
Mom										

Exercise 2 7

Listen to the conversation again and cross off (✗) the things each person *cannot* do.

Speaking task one

Take turns asking and answering questions with Student B. If you have blanks, ask Student B questions and fill in the blanks. Listen to Student B and answer the questions.

Example

| Student A | Does Mary know how to sing? | Student B | Can she play the piano? |
| Student B | Yes, she does. | Student A | Uh-uh. |

Memo

Ask and answer in *different* ways, but only write "yes," "no" or "a little" in the blanks.

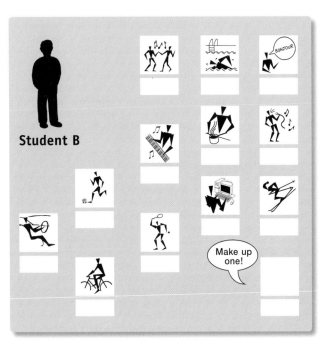

Speaking task two   Do this exercise with everyone.

The teacher will give you one of the boxes below. Walk around the classroom and ask yes/no questions. Write the name of one person in each blank.

Memo

- Ask and answer in *different* ways.
- Change partners after asking *one* question.
- Give true answers!

Example

Student A	Do you know how to ski?	Student B	Can you play chess?
Student B	Yes, I do.	Student C	No, I can't.

1 Find someone who:

- can ride a skateboard.
- knows how to ski.
- *can't* ride a bicycle.
- can play the piano.
- knows how to use a fax machine.

2 Find someone who:

- knows how to ride a horse.
- knows how to play baseball.
- can dive into a swimming pool.
- can play chess.
- *doesn't* know how to fix a flat tire.

3 Find someone who:

- can sing a song in English.
- knows how to row a boat.
- can play the guitar.
- *can't* swim.
- knows how to play basketball.

4 Find someone who:

- knows how to surf.
- *can't* draw pictures.
- knows how to snowboard.
- can ice-skate.
- knows how to play volleyball.

5 Find someone who:

- can drive a truck.
- *can't* cook.
- knows how to read music.
- can play badminton.
- knows how to make cookies.

6 Find someone who:

- knows how to play tennis.
- can type very fast.
- can water ski.
- knows how to scuba dive.
- *can't* sing.

7 Find someone who:

- can play golf.
- can bowl very well.
- *doesn't* know how to fish.
- knows how to read a map well.
- knows how to play ping-pong.

8 Find someone who:

- knows how to drive.
- can play soccer.
- knows how to sew.
- *can't* dance.
- knows how to throw a Frisbee.

Homework

Fill in the blanks in the sentences below and write the answers in the puzzle on page 10.

Fill in the blanks in the sentences below and write the answers in the puzzle on page 10.

Memo
Look at the answers in the box on page 10 for help.

ACROSS →

2 He can play baseball well. He hits a homerun every game!

6 I can't play _____ well because I'm not tall and I can't get the ball in the basket.

7 She knows how to play the electric _____ like a rock and roll star!

8 I know how to play _____, but I always lose my queen when I play.

10 We can't play _____ at the beach today because I can't find the rackets or the net.

12 Does your son know how to _____? He can come to our pool party on Sunday.

13 He can _____ pictures of animals beautifully.

14 My brother can play _____ very well. He always scores lots of goals.

15 I can't _____. If a button comes off my shirt, my mother fixes it.

16 She can play _____ very well. She can jump high and hit the ball over the net every time.

DOWN ↓

1 I don't know how to _____ any musical instruments, but I can sing.

2 The little boy can't _____ because the ball is too heavy and the pins are too far.

3 She has a great voice! She can really _____ beautifully.

4 Look at those beautiful colors! That artist can _____ very well.

5 Do you know how to _____ a skateboard?

8 She knows how to _____ Chinese food. It's my favorite!

9 I don't like snow and I hate cold weather, so I don't know how to _____

11 That ballerina can _____ beautifully.

12 My brother can't _____ very well. He always uses a dictionary when he writes.

13 Does your sister really know how to _____ a truck?

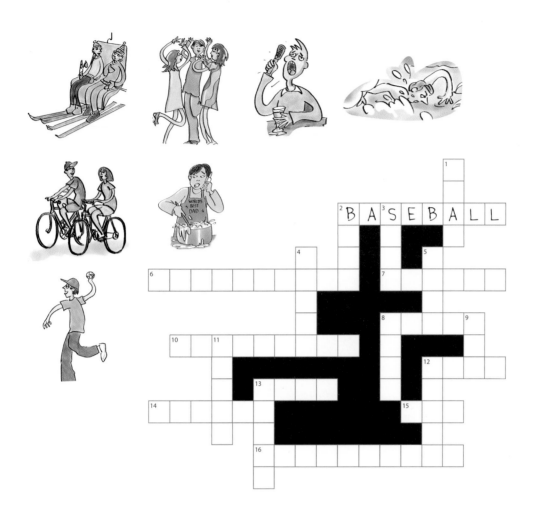

Homework review
Work in a group of three students.

Student A
Read the sentences from page 9 to your partners. (Say "blank" for the answer you wrote.)

Students B and C
Listen to the sentences (with your book closed). Take turns and guess the answer for the "blank." (If you cannot guess the answer, look at the puzzle above to find it.)

Memo
- Do this exercise in the next lesson if you have time.
- Each one take a turn as Student A and read seven sentences.

Language focus

Can	you / they	sing?		Yes,	I / they	can.		No,	I / they	can't.
	he / she	speak Spanish?		Yeah,	he / she			Nah,	he / she	
		play tennis?		Uh huh.				Uh-uh.		

A little.
Yes, but only a little.
Yeah, but not very well.

Do	you / they	know how to	ski?		Yes,	I / they	do.		No,	I / they	don't.
			use a computer?		Yeah,	he / she	does.		Nah,	he / she	doesn't.
Does	he / she		play the piano?		Uh huh.				Uh-uh.		

10

Warm-up exercises

Exercise 1

Write the woman's question.

I work for Riverdale Animal Rescue.

?

Exercise 2 🔘 8

Listen to the following conversation. Then practice it with a partner.

Memo

Always look at the person you are speaking to. Don't look down at the page!

Amanda	Who's that new guy?
Bernice	His name's Andrew, and he can speak five languages.
Amanda	Wow! Where's he from?
Bernice	He's from Canada.
Amanda	How old is he? Do you know?
Bernice	He's twenty-five or twenty-six, I think, and he's single!

Exercise 3

Practice the conversation a few more times. Each time, use the ideas below or your own ideas.

- Harold
- four languages
- England
- twenty-nine

- Yoshi
- three languages
- Japan
- twenty-four

- Martin
- six languages
- Germany
- twenty-seven

Look at page 15

Language focus

11

Listening task

Exercise 1 9–11

Listen to the conversations (1–3) and write the number of each conversation next to the correct picture.

Exercise 2 9–11

Listen again and write the answers to the questions.

Conversation 1	Conversation 2	Conversation 3
What does she do?	What does she do?	Where is she from?
Who does she work for?	What is she studying?	Which part?
Where does she work?	What school does she go to?	What does she do?

Student B, turn to page 90

Speaking task one

Take turns with Student B asking and answering questions. Ask Student B for information to fill in the blanks in the chart.

Example

| Student B | Where's Cathy from? |
| Student A | She's from the United States. |

Memo

Answer in full sentences, but only write *notes* in your blanks.

	Name	Cathy	Bill	Lee	Yoon-Hee	Mike and Lily	Student B
	Where / from?	the United States		China		Canada	
	Which part?	New York		Beijing		Quebec	
	Age?	33		22		both 24	
	Married?	yes		no		yes	
	Children?	one girl		no		no	
	Occupation?	an English teacher		a student		students	
W O R K	Who / for?	Cosmos English Institute					
	Where / work?	Tokyo					
S T U D Y	What / studying?			English		Medicine	
	School?			Queens College		University of Milan	

13

Speaking task two Do Exercise 1 alone and Exercise 2 with everyone.

Exercise 1

Circle one item to complete each sentence. Use these as *your answers* in Exercise 2.

I'm from ...	• New Zealand.	• England.	• Australia.	• the United States.
I'm a ...	• taxi driver.	• pilot.	• doctor.	• chef.
I'm ...	• 24.	• 28.	• 30.	• 32.
I'm ...	• single.	• married.		
I ...	• have children.	• don't have any children.		

Exercise 2

Walk around the classroom and ask yes/no questions or *Wh-* questions. Write the name of one classmate in each box. When you have four different names in a line, shout "Bingo!" and sit down.

Example

| **Student A** | Where are you from? | **Student A** | Are you from England? |
| **Student B** | I'm from New Zealand. | **Student C** | Yes, I am! |

_____ name is the same age as you.	_____ name is from New Zealand.	_____ name is a taxi driver.	_____ name doesn't have any children.
_____ name has children.	_____ name is a chef.	_____ name comes from the United States.	_____ name is married.
_____ name is from England.	_____ name is older than you.	_____ name has children.	_____ name is a pilot.
_____ name is a doctor.	_____ name is single.	_____ name is younger than you.	_____ name is from Australia.

Homework

Write six questions with answers about the personal information of someone you know (a neighbor, a friend or a family member, etc.).

1   France

Japan

Italy

2

3

4

5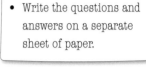

6

Homework review   Do this exercise with a partner.

Student A
Find out who your partner wrote about and ask the questions (1–6) that you wrote for homework.

Student B
Answer your partner's questions without looking at the answers that you wrote for homework.

Example

Student A	Who did you write about?	Student A	Where's he from?
Student B	I wrote about my neighbor, Richard.	Student B	He's from England.

Language focus

Where are you from?	→	I'm from England.
Where in / Which part of England?	→	London.

What		do?	→	I'm a salesperson.
Who	do you	work for?	→	I work for IBM.
Where		work?		in Richmond.

What do you do?	→	I'm a student.
What are you studying?	→	I'm studying Economics.
What school do you go to?		I go to the University of Colorado.

Private questions

How old are you?	→	I'm twenty-five.	
Are you married?	→	Yes, I am.	No, I'm not.
Do you have any children?		Yes, I do.	No, I don't.

15

3 TIME TO LEARN
Time and date

Warm-up exercises

Exercise 1

Write the woman's question.

Exercise 2 12

Listen to the following conversation. Then practice it with a partner.

> **Memo**
>
> Always look at the person you are speaking to. Don't look down at the page!

Elsie	I'm tired of waiting. Where is he?
Seth	I don't know. He said half past two.
Elsie	What time is it?
Seth	It's quarter after three. What's today's date?
Elsie	It's Thursday the fifth. Why?
Seth	Oh. He said the sixth. Sorry.

Exercise 3

Practice the conversation a few more times. Each time, use the ideas below or your own ideas.

Look at page 21
Language focu

Listening task

Listen to the conversations (1–8) and write the number of each conversation next to the correct picture.

 ☐

 ☐

 ☐

 ☐

 ☐

 ☐

 ☐

 ☐

Listen to the conversations again and write the two times or dates in each conversation.

> **Memo**
> Write only *numbers* for the times and dates, such as 8:30 or 2/9.

1 opens ☐
  closes ☐

2 leaves ☐
  returns ☐

3 brother's ☐
  sister's ☐

4 opens ☐
  closes ☐

5 begins ☐
  ends ☐

6 breakfast ☐
  lunch ☐

7 starts ☐
  finishes ☐

8 opens ☐
  closes ☐

Student B, turn to page 91

Speaking task one

Exercise 1

Look at each clock (1–12) and tell Student B the time.

> **Example**
>
> **Student B**   Excuse me, what time is it?
> **Student A**   It's a quarter after seven.

Memo

Use different ways to ask and tell the time.

Vocabulary

- exactly
- on the dot
- past
- after
- to
- before
- a quarter
- half past

Exercise 2

Ask Student B the time and draw the hands on each clock (1–12).

> **Example**
>
> **Student A**   Pardon me, do you know the time?
> **Student B**   It's half past twelve.

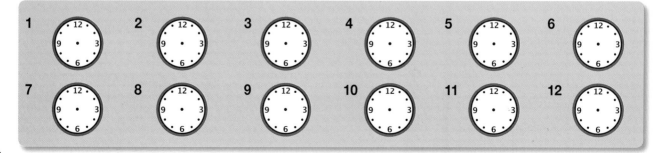

Exercise 3 Do this exercise with a partner.

Ask Student B for the birthdays of the people below and fill in the blanks under "Birthday." Tell Student B the birthdays of the people below. Then write every name under the correct zodiac sign in the chart on the right.

> **Memo**
> Use different ways to ask and tell the date.

Example

Student B When's Mary's birthday?	**Student A** What date's Jane's birthday?
Student A It's December the twenty-seventh.	**Student B** It's the fifteenth of February.

Name	Birthday
Mary	12/27
Jane	
Alan	
John	
Mark	5/12
Ellen	
Milly	7/20
Loni	5/22
Helen	
Marty	8/1
Mike	
Ronnie	9/3

Capricorn December 22 – January 19 — name / name

Aquarius January 20 – February 18 — name / name

Pisces February 19 – March 20 — name / name

Aries March 21 – April 19 — name / name

Taurus April 20 – May 20 — name / name

Gemini May 21 – June 20 — name / name

Cancer June 21 – July 22 — name / name

Leo July 23 – August 22 — name / name

Virgo August 23 – September 22 — name / name

Libra September 23 – October 22 — name / name

Scorpio October 23 – November 21 — name / name

Sagittarius November 22 – December 21 — name / name

Exercise 4 Do this exercise with everyone.

Walk around the classroom and ask your classmates for their birthdays. Find one person for each zodiac sign and write his or her name and birthday in the blank.

Group B, turn to page 93

Speaking task two   Do this exercise with everyone.

The teacher will divide the class into two halves, Group A and Group B, and give each student in Group A one of the boxes below. Walk around the classroom and ask students in Group B for the information to write in your box.

Example

Student A	It's a quarter after twelve in New York. What time is it in London?
Student B	It's a quarter after five in London.
Student A	When's St. Patrick's Day in Ireland?
Student B	It's the seventeenth of March.

Memo
- Do not show your box to anyone!
- *Group B* students may stay in their seats.

---

1 Find someone who knows this information:

New York  London

- Independence Day in the United States
- Bastille Day in France

2 Find someone who knows this information:

New York London

- St. Patrick's Day in Ireland
- Australia Day in Australia

---

3 Find someone who knows this information:

Paris London

- Canada Day in Canada
- Boxing Day in the United Kingdom

4 Find someone who knows this information:

Paris Sydney

- Independence Day in Russia
- Children's Day in Japan

---

5 Find someone who knows this information:

Tokyo Quebec

- National Day in Singapore
- Republic Day in India

6 Find someone who knows this information:

Tokyo Rome

- Constitution Memorial Day in Japan
- National Day in China

---

7 Find someone who knows this information:

Seoul Beijing

- National Day in Switzerland
- Constitution Day in Thailand

8 Find someone who knows this information:

Seoul Bangkok

- Memorial Day in the United States
- Thanksgiving Day in Canada

Homework

Exercise 1

Choose any six of the clocks below and write out the time for each. Use these words: *after, past, to, before, quarter to* and *half past.*

Example

It is a quarter to one.

1	2	3	4	5	6
7	8	9	10	11	12

Exercise 2

Write out the birthdates of six of your classmates from Exercise 4 on page 19 or 92.

Example

• May the twenty-third
• the second of February

Homework review **Do this exercise with everyone.**

Walk around and talk to your classmates. For each of the times and dates you wrote for homework, find someone who wrote the same time or date as you and write that person's name next to your sentence.

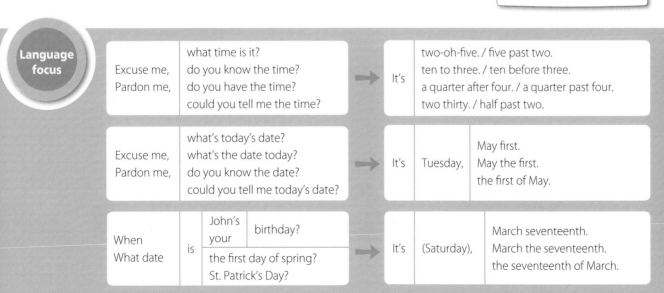

Language focus

		what time is it?			It's	two-oh-five. / five past two.
Excuse me, Pardon me,		do you know the time? do you have the time? could you tell me the time?		→		ten to three. / ten before three. a quarter after four. / a quarter past four. two thirty. / half past two.

		what's today's date?			It's	Tuesday,	May first.
Excuse me, Pardon me,		what's the date today? do you know the date? could you tell me today's date?		→			May the first. the first of May.

When What date	is	John's your	birthday?	→	It's	(Saturday),	March seventeenth.
		the first day of spring? St. Patrick's Day?					March the seventeenth. the seventeenth of March.

4 DAY TO DAY
Daily routine

Warm-up exercises

Exercise 1

Write the boy's question.

Exercise 2 21

Listen to the following conversation. Then practice it with a partner.

> **Memo**
>
> Always look at the person you are speaking to. Don't look down at the page!

Mark	How's your new roommate?
Russ	He's crazy! He gets up at half past four every day.
Mark	Four thirty in the morning? Why?
Russ	He exercises for two hours before breakfast.
Mark	Does he wake you up?
Russ	No, nothing wakes me up at four thirty!

Exercise 3

Practice the conversation a few more times. Each time, use the ideas below or your own ideas.

 /    /

plays guitar   watches TV   listens to music

Look at page 26
Language foc

Listening task

Exercise 1 22

Listen to Chris talk about his daily schedule and his wife's schedule. Number the activities from 1 to 10 in the order they are mentioned.

Exercise 2 22

Listen again and write the time mentioned on each picture (1–10).

Exercise 3 22

Listen again and write the verb mentioned for each picture (1–10).

Student B, turn to page 94

Speaking task one

Take turns asking and answering questions with Student B. If you have blanks, ask Student B questions and fill in the blanks. Listen to Student B and answer the questions.

Example

Student B	What does Bob do?	Student A	Where does he have lunch?
Student A	He's a truck driver.	Student B	He has lunch at a coffee shop.

Memo

Answer in full sentences, but only write *notes* in your blanks.

Name / Occupation	🏠→🚶	🚶→🏢	🚶→🍽	🪑 MENU	🏠←🚶	🌙
Bob — truck driver	(clock)	(clock)			(clock)	🚶→ ♟♟♟♟♟
Ted	(clock)	(clock)	in a restaurant	with his customers	(clock)	
Carol — office assistant	(clock)	(clock)			(clock)	📺 🚶
Alice	(clock)	(clock)		with other nurses	(clock)	🎸 📖
Jack — taxi driver	(clock)	(clock)	at a cafe		(clock)	
Betty	(clock)	(clock)	at home	alone	(clock)	
Student B	(clock)	(clock)			(clock)	

QUESTIONS

- What does Bob do?
- What time does he leave home?
- What time does he get to work?
- Where does he have lunch?
- Who does he have lunch with?
- What time does he get home?
- What does he do in the evening?

24

Speaking task two

Student A
Guess the answer to each question about Student B in the box below and tell Student B what you think. Then check (✓) if you are right or wrong.

Student B
Listen to Student A's guesses about your daily routine and tell Student A if each guess is right or wrong.

> **Memo**
> - Find a *new* partner for Speaking task two.
> - Change roles as Student A and Student B, and do the exercise again.

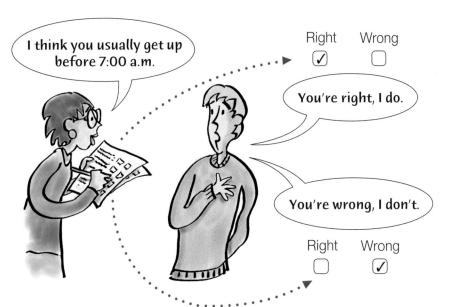

I think you usually get up before 7:00 a.m.

Right Wrong
 ✓   ☐

You're right, I do.

You're wrong, I don't.

Right Wrong
 ☐   ✓

Does Student B usually ...	Right	Wrong
... get up before or after 7:00 a.m.?	☐	☐
... get dressed before or after breakfast?	☐	☐
... leave home before or after 8:00 a.m.?	☐	☐
... have lunch before or after 12:15?	☐	☐
... eat lunch alone or with someone?	☐	☐
... get home before or after 5:00 p.m.?	☐	☐
... eat dinner alone or with someone?	☐	☐
... have dinner before or after 7:00 p.m.?	☐	☐
... watch TV alone or with someone?	☐	☐
... stay home or go out on Saturday night?	☐	☐
... sleep late or get up early on Sunday?	☐	☐
... go to bed before or after 11:15 p.m.?	☐	☐
Total:		

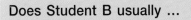

Homework

Use one of the pictures from each set (1–6) and write a sentence about the daily routine of the woman. (Write all six sentences about the same woman.)

Memo

Write the sentences on a separate sheet of paper.

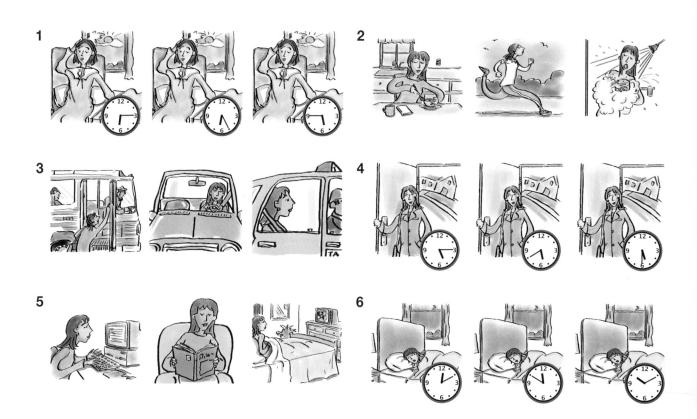

Homework review Do this exercise with everyone.

Walk around and talk to your classmates. Ask and answer questions about the sets of pictures (1–6) above. For each set, find someone who used the *same picture* as you, and write that person's name next to your sentence.

Memo

• Do this exercise in the next lesson if you have time.

• If you cannot find anyone, write "no one."

Language focus

What	do	you / they	do	after school?	→	I / We / They	go	to the library.
	does	he / she		on Sunday?		He / She	goes	to the park.

Who	do	you / they	have lunch with?	→	I / We / They	have lunch	with friends.
	does	he / she			He / She	has lunch	with classmates.

Do	you / they	get up before 7:00?	→	Yes,	I /we / they	do.
		watch TV after dinner?			he / she	does.
Does	he / she			No,	I / we / they	don't.
					he / she	doesn't.

Review exercises

Exercise 1

The teacher will give you one of the pictures (1–4) below. There is a question for each picture. Write an answer for the question.

1

Man	Tony?! Do you know what time it is, Tony?

2

Woman	Oh, dear! Do you know how to swim?

3

Girl	What do you usually do in the summer?

4

Doorman	How old are you guys?

Exercise 2

Read your answer to the class. Do *not* read the question. The class will guess your picture.

Listening task

Exercise 1 23–27

Listen to the conversations (1–5) with your *book closed*. Then open your book and write the number of each conversation next to the correct picture.

Memo

- You can take notes as you listen.
- There is no conversation for one picture.

Exercise 2 23–27

Listen again and write the *keywords* next to each picture.

Memo

Keywords are important words that tell you which picture to choose.

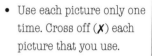
Speaking task one   Play this game with one "caller" and two "players."

Choose any picture below and make up a statement or question. Tell the players the sentence.
Continue to choose pictures and tell the players sentences until one player shouts "Bingo!"

Example

    Caller   I can play the piano a little.

    Caller   Who do you usually have lunch with?

     Caller   She usually gets home at half past ten.
(continue)

> **Memo**
> - Use each picture only one time. Cross off (✗) each picture that you use.
> - You can use two or three pictures in one sentence if you like.
> - Say each sentence two times.

Speaking task two   Do this exercise with everyone.

The teacher will give you one of the boxes below. Walk around the classroom and ask yes/no or *Wh-* questions. Write the name of one person in each blank. (If you cannot find anyone, write "no one.")

Memo
- Try to find four *different* people for the four blanks.
- Change partners after asking *one* question.
- Give true answers!

Example

Student A	Do you drive to school?	Student A	How do you get to
Student B	Yes, I do.		school?
		Student C	I take the bus.

1 Find someone who:
- drives to school.
- reads on the way to school.
- comes to school by bus.
- takes less than 15 minutes to come to school.

2 Find someone who:
- eats breakfast at school.
- goes to the library after school.
- meets friends before class.
- listens to music on the way to school.

3 Find someone who:
- comes to school by subway.
- brings lunch to school.
- always comes to school early.
- reads the newspaper before class.

4 Find someone who:
- studies on the way to school.
- does homework in the library.
- does homework in class.
- takes more than one hour to get to school.

5 Find someone who:
- walks to school.
- comes to school with friends.
- eats on the way to school.
- drinks coffee on the way to school.

6 Find someone who:
- rides a bicycle to school.
- often gets to school late.
- drinks water in the classroom.
- comes to school by bus *and* subway.

7 Find someone who:
- comes to school alone.
- meets friends after school.
- sleeps on the way to school.
- does homework on the way to school.

8 Find someone who:
- eats in the classroom.
- lives very close to school.
- comes to school in a friend's car.
- listens to English CDs on the way to school.

Caller, turn to page 96

Language game

Play this game with two to four "players" and one "caller."

Take turns choosing two numbers (1–24) from the grid below. Each number is a question or an answer. The caller will read each sentence that you choose.

Choose one number, listen to the caller read the sentence and then choose another number. Try to match a question with the answer. Do not write any notes. Just listen!

Continue until all the questions and answers have been matched. The player with the most matches wins!

> **Memo**
> * Cross off (✗) all matched numbers and circle *your* matches.
> * Look at this page only!
> * The teacher may let you write notes on the numbers.

Example	

Player A	Number 4.	**Player B**	Number 23.
Caller	"What does he do?"	**Caller**	"He's a photographer."
Player A	Number 11.	**Player B**	Number 4.
Caller	"No, he isn't." They don't match!	**Caller**	"What does he do?" They match!

1	2	3	4	5	6
7	8	9	10	11	12
13	14	15	16	17	18
19	20	21	22	23	24

6 WHERE DOES IT GO?

Location and moving things

Warm-up exercises

Exercise 1

Write the firefighter's question.

What? Oh, it's in the backyard.

?

Exercise 2 28

Listen to the following conversation. Then practice it with a partner.

Memo

Always look at the person you are speaking to. Don't look down at the page!

Miki	OK, where does that plant go?
Felicia	Oh, put it on the windowsill.
Miki	How about this lamp?
Felicia	That goes on the desk.
Miki	Where's the desk?
Felicia	The desk? Oh, it's still in the truck.

Exercise 3

Practice the conversation a few more times. Each time, use the ideas below or your own ideas.

camera   shelf   dishes   cabinet   umbrellas   closet

Look at page **37**

Language focus

32

Listening task

Listen to the directions and move the objects around the room.

Example

"Take the TV remote control and put it on the speaker, next to the TV."

> **Memo**
>
> To move an object, circle it, draw a line to the new place and make an "✗."

Vocabulary

- pick up
- take
- from
- put
- it
- them
- on
- next to
- camera
- chess set
- magazines
- photo album
- pillow
- sunglasses
- DVD
- wine glasses
- bookcase
- coffee table
- desk
- fireplace
- floor
- lamp
- sofa
- speaker

Listen and circle "true" or "false" for each sentence (1–8).

> **Memo**
>
> Answer "true" or "false" about the *new* position of each object (marked with an "✗").

| **1** | true | false | **2** | true | false | **3** | true | false | **4** | true | false |
| **5** | true | false | **6** | true | false | **7** | true | false | **8** | true | false |

Speaking task one   Do Exercise 1 alone and Exercise 2 with everyone.

Exercise 1

Your teacher will give you one or more objects to "put away" in the house (on pages 34 and 35). Put each object somewhere in the living room or kitchen. You can write the number of the object on the picture or draw the object on the picture.

Memo

Use an arrow (→) to put an object *inside* something, such as a cabinet.

1	2	3	4	5
laptop computer	frying pan	notebook	wine glasses	remote control

6	7	8	9	10
teacup	magazines	cell phone	teapot	photo album

Vocabulary

- bookcase
- coffee table
- desk
- fireplace
- floor
- lamp
- sofa
- speaker
- stereo cabinet

Exercise 2

Walk around the classroom and ask and answer questions. Find out where every object goes and put away each one. You can answer questions about all your classmates' objects that you put away. For any others, answer, "Sorry, I don't know."

Example

Student A	Where does the teapot go?	Student B	Where do the sunglasses go?
Student B	It goes on the kitchen table.	Student A	They go in the desk drawer.

11	12	13	14	15
sunglasses	DVD	dictionary	toaster	camera

16	17	18	19	20
calculator	oven mitt	CDs	plant	radio

Vocabulary

• cabinet
• counter
• dishwasher
• hook
• kitchen table
• microwave (oven)
• refrigerator
• sink
• stove

Speaking task two

Some of the objects are in different places in Student B's picture. Take turns asking questions about location and telling each other where to move the objects to make the pictures the same. (Only move objects that are in different places.)

Example

Student A	Where's the broom?	Student B	Where are the skis?
Student B	It's on the floor, next to the workbench.	Student A	They're next to the side door, on the right.
Student A	That's the same.	Student B	That's different. Pick them up and put them ...

Memo

To move an object, cross it out and draw it in the new place.

Vocabulary

OBJECTS

- gas can
- lawn mower
- patio umbrella
- ladder
- lawn chairs
- bicycles
- golf clubs
- paintbrushes
- paint cans
- rake
- hose
- garbage cans
- saw
- tennis rackets
- shovel
- tires
- toolbox
- screens

LOCATIONS

- cabinet
- garage door
- side door
- shelf
- workbench
- corner

Homework

Write a sentence about each item (1–8) below. Write where each item usually goes in your home. (Write about the room and the place in the room.)

Example

- My dictionary goes in my bedroom, on the desk.
- My shoes go in the living room, in the closet.

Memo
Write the sentences on a separate sheet of paper.

1
jacket

2
school books

3
alarm clock

4
shoes

5
camera

6
CDs

7
dictionary

8
your own idea

Homework review   Do this exercise with everyone.

Walk around and talk to your classmates. Ask and answer questions about the items (1–8) above. Find someone who puts each item away in the same place as you and write that person's name next to your sentence.

Memo
- Do this exercise in the next lesson if you have time.
- If you cannot find anyone, write "no one."

Example

Student B   Where does your dictionary go?
Student A   It goes in my bedroom, on the desk.

Language focus

Where	is	the phone book?		It's	on the desk, by the telephone.
	are	the pens?		They're	in the drawer, next to the dictionary.

Where	does	the teapot	go?	It	goes	behind the sink, on the shelf.
		the sugar				on the table, in front of the toaster.
	do	the magazines		They	go	under the coffee table.
		the sunglasses				between the radio and the clock.

Pick up	the sugar bowl	and put	it	on the counter, next to the coffee pot.
Take	the wine glasses		them	in the cabinet over the sink, on the right.

37

Warm-up exercises

Exercise 1

Write the man's answer.

Pardon me, how can I get to the Dune Hotel from here?

Exercise 2　 45

Listen to the following conversation. Then practice it with a partner.

Memo

Always look at the person you are speaking to. Don't look down at the page!

Man	Excuse me. How can I get to the subway station from here?
Woman	The subway? Go straight for two blocks.
Man	Straight, two blocks.
Woman	Turn right, and it's on your left. It's next to the bank.
Man	So, that's straight for two blocks, turn right, and it's on the left, next to the bank.
Woman	That's right.

Exercise 3

Practice the conversation a few more times. Each time, ask for and give directions to a place on the map.

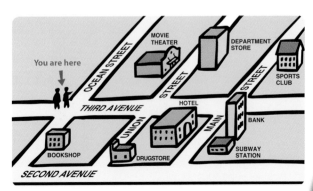

You are here

Look at page 42
Language fo

Listening task 46–50

Listen to the directions in each conversation (1–5) and write the name of each place on the correct building.

Memo

The people speaking in each conversation are numbered (1–5).

Vocabulary

- bank
- doctor's office
- feed store
- general store
- hardware store
- hotel
- saloon
- sheriff's office
- telegraph office

Speaking task one   Do Exercise 1 alone and Exercise 2 with a partner.

Exercise 1

Match each place on the left (1–7) with one sentence about its location on the right.

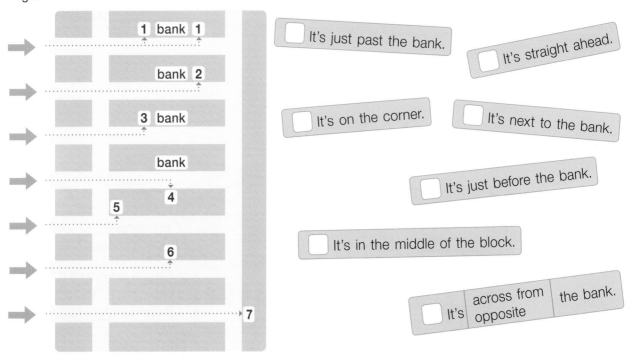

Exercise 2

For each place below, tell your partner the location. Do *not* give directions and do *not* say the name of the place. Your partner will guess the name of the place.

Example

Student B	It's next to the subway station.
Student A	It's the pub.
Student B	That's right!

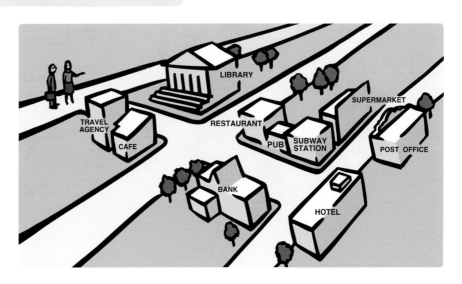

Speaking task two

Exercise 1

Ask Student B for directions to each place below. Write the name of each place on the building.

PLACES

- the post office
- Bell's Piano School
- Al's Jazz Club
- the French restaurant
- the fire station
- Buck's Hardware
- Ryan's Pub
- the First Central Bank
- the Health Food Store
- Walden's Bookstore

Memo

Go to each new place from the previous place: go to #2 from #1, then go to #3 from #2 and so on.

Exercise 2

Look at the map and give directions to Student B. (Student B does not know the names of the places in red.)

Homework

Write directions to go from a bus stop or a train station to your home. Draw a simple map for the directions.

Example

Go west and turn left at the first corner.
Go straight for two blocks and turn right.
My house is the second house on the left.
It is across from the school.

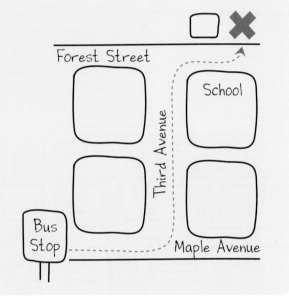

Homework review Do this exercise with a partner.

Take turns giving each other the directions that you wrote for homework. Write down your partner's directions and draw a simple map.

Language focus

Excuse me. Pardon me.	Where is the subway station? Do you know where the library is? Could you tell me where the bus stop is? How can I get to the post office from here?

Go (straight)	up down	this street Tenth Avenue	for	one block three blocks	and turn	right. left.
			and turn	right left	at the	first corner. third corner.

It's	next to just past just before across from opposite	the bank.	It's	on the corner. in the middle of the block. straight ahead.	
				on the	right. left.

8 ALL DRESSED UP
Describing people

Warm-up exercises

Exercise 1

Write the woman's answer.

Exercise 2 51

Listen to the following conversation. Then practice it with a partner.

> **Memo**
> Always look at the person you are speaking to. Don't look down at the page!

Pat	So, how old's your cousin?
Niki	He's nineteen, and he's a college student.
Pat	What does he look like?
Niki	He's tall and thin, and he has long black hair.
Pat	Is he good-looking?
Niki	Yes, he is.

Exercise 3

Practice the conversation a few more times.
Each time, use the men on the right or your own ideas.

Look at page 47
Language focus

43

Listening task

Exercise 1   52

Listen to the conversation and write the correct number (1–8) on each person in the picture.

1 **Andrea**	2 **Robert**
– white skirt – striped blouse – short, curly hair	

3 **Mark**	4 **Albert**

5 **Melanie**	6 **Amy**

7 **Lee**	8 **Rod**

Exercise 2   52

Listen again and write notes about each person's description.

Student B, turn to page 99

Speaking task one

Take turns asking and answering questions about the people (1–16) below. Ask about people you do not have names for. Fill in the blanks with the correct names.

Example

Student A	What's that woman's name?
Student B	Which woman?
Student A	She's tall, and she has curly black hair, and she's wearing a long dress.
Student B	Her name's Ruth.

Memo

- Ask only about appearance.
- Sit face to face with your partner.

1		2 Terry	3	4 Ken
5		6	7 Patty	8 Warren
9		10 Alice	11	12 Andrew
13 Walter		14 Arthur	15	16

Student B, turn to page 100

Speaking task two

The men on the stage below are different from the men in Student B's picture. Take turns asking and answering yes/no questions about each man and circle the differences.

Example

Student A	Is the first man wearing black shoes?
Student B	No, he isn't. He's wearing boots.
Student A	That's different!

> **Memo**
> - Only the six men on the stage are different.
> - Start with the man on the left.

Homework

Find a large picture of an interesting person in a magazine or newspaper. Write a description of the person. (Write three or more sentences.) Cut out the picture and bring it to class.

Memo

- Write the sentences on a separate sheet of paper.
- Use a large picture that is big enough for the class to see on the board.

Example

- She is tall and thin.
- She has long, blonde hair.
- She is wearing a long, gold dress.

Homework review   Work in a group of three or four students.

The teacher will put everyone's picture on the board and number each picture.

Memo

- Do this exercise in the next lesson if you have time.
- All questions must be about appearance.

Student A

Choose any picture on the board. (It does not have to be your picture.) Answer questions ("yes" or "no") until someone guesses the picture.

Students B, C and D

Take turns asking Student A yes/no questions about people in the pictures until you can guess the correct picture.

Example

Student B	Is the person a man or a woman?
Student A	A woman.
Student C	Does she have short hair?
Student A	No, she doesn't.

Student D	Is she wearing a long, gold dress?
Student A	Yes, she is.
Student D	Is it picture number five?
Student A	Yes!

Language focus

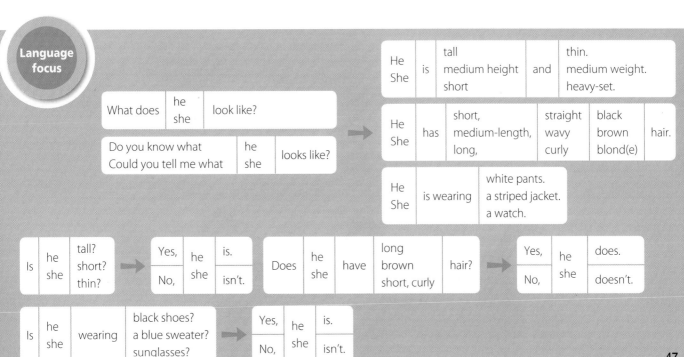

| What does | he / she | look like? |

| Do you know what / Could you tell me what | he / she | looks like? |

| He / She | is | tall / medium height / short | and | thin. / medium weight. / heavy-set. |

| He / She | has | short, / medium-length, / long, | straight / wavy / curly | black / brown / blond(e) | hair. |

| He / She | is wearing | white pants. / a striped jacket. / a watch. |

| Is | he / she | tall? / short? / thin? | → | Yes, / No, | he / she | is. / isn't. |

| Does | he / she | have | long / brown / short, curly | hair? | → | Yes, / No, | he / she | does. / doesn't. |

| Is | he / she | wearing | black shoes? / a blue sweater? / sunglasses? | → | Yes, / No, | he / she | is. / isn't. |

47

9 FAMILY PORTRAIT

Talking about family

Warm-up exercises

Exercise 1

Write the girl's answer.

Do you have any brothers or sisters?

Exercise 2 🔘 53

Listen to the following conversation. Then practice it with a partner.

> **Memo**
> Always look at the person you are speaking to. Don't look down at the page!

Mary	Hi, Gina. Who are all those people?
Gina	My family. I have, like, sixteen cousins.
Mary	Sixteen? How many aunts and uncles do you have?
Gina	Well, my mother has four sisters and one brother, and my father has two brothers.
Mary	Man, that's a lot.
Gina	Yeah, right, and my sister-in-law has five brothers!

Exercise 3

Practice the conversation a few more times. Each time, describe a different family.

Look at page 54
Language focus

Exercise 4   Do this exercise with a partner.

Take turns asking and answering questions about Alfred's family.

Example

Student A	Who's Jim Barton?
Student B	He's Alfred's uncle.
Student B	What's Alfred's cousin's name?
Student A	His cousin's name is Sally Connor.

Albert Ames   Melba Ames   Bob Barton   Mary Barton

Robert Connor   Diane Connor   Allan Ames   Susan Ames   Jim Barton   Bob Ellis   Grace Ellis

Sally Connor   Harry Dell   Mary Dell   Alfred Ames   Jean Ames   Carol Ellis

Bruce Dell   Pam Dell   Arnold Ames   Debby Ames

Vocabulary

- grandfather
- grandmother
- mother
- father
- brother
- sister
- niece
- nephew
- husband
- wife
- son
- daughter
- uncle
- aunt
- cousin
- mother-in-law
- father-in-law
- brother-in-law
- sister-in-law

Listening task

Exercise 1 54

Listen to the conversation and write the number (1–7) of each person on the picture.

Exercise 2 54

Listen again and fill in the other information in the chart (*relation*, *age* and *occupation*).

> **M e m o**
> * For "relation" (to Jean) write "brother," "aunt," "cousin," etc.
> * You do not hear *everyone's* age or occupation.

	1	2	3	4	5	6	7
Name	Paul	Amy	Bobby	Tina	Pamela	Phil	Mary
Relation*							
Age							
Occupation							

*Relation to Jean

Speaking task one

Exercise 1

Ask Student B questions. Write the answers on the questionnaire.

1 Name:			2 Age:		
3 Occupation:			4 Married: Yes ☐ No ☐		

	Name	Age	Married	Occupation	Lives in
5 Brothers:					
6 Sisters:					

Exercise 2

Answer Student B's questions about "your family" on this page. These are pictures of you and your brothers and sisters.

Diane

My younger sister is a high school student. She is 17 years old. She lives in Boston with my parents.

Carol

My older sister is married and has two children. She is 24 and lives in Dallas. She is a homemaker.

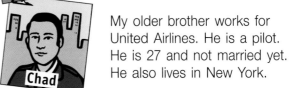

Student A

Pat

I am a taxi driver, and I live in New York. I am 22 and single.

Bob

My younger brother is 19 and he is in college. He also lives with my parents in Boston.

Chad

My older brother works for United Airlines. He is a pilot. He is 27 and not married yet. He also lives in New York.

Exercise 3

Ask Student B questions about his or her *actual* brothers and sisters. Write the answers on the questionnaire.

> **Memo**
> If you or your partner have no brothers or sisters, talk about cousins.

1 Name:			2 Age:		
3 Occupation:			4 Married: Yes ☐ No ☐		

	Name	Age	Married	Occupation	Lives in
5 Brothers:					
6 Sisters:					

Exercise 4

Answer Student B's questions about yourself and your *actual* brothers and sisters. (Just answer, do not write!)

Speaking task two

Student A
Tell Student B something true or not true about a member of your family. Student B will guess if you are telling the truth or not. Then check (✓) if Student B's guess is right or wrong.

Student B
Listen to Student A's statements about his or her family members. Do you think each statement is true or not? Tell Student A if you believe it or do not believe it.

Memo
- Find a *new* partner for Speaking task two.
- Change roles as Student A and Student B, and do the exercise again.

Tell Student B about your ...

	Student B is	
	Right	Wrong
... brother(s).	☐	☐
... sister(s).	☐	☐
... aunt(s).	☐	☐
... uncle(s).	☐	☐
... cousin(s).	☐	☐
... niece(s).	☐	☐
... nephew(s).	☐	☐
... brother(s)-in-law/sister(s)-in-law.	☐	☐
... grandmother(s).	☐	☐
... grandfather(s).	☐	☐
Total:	▭	▭

Memo

If you don't have a niece or brother-in-law, etc., tell a lie!

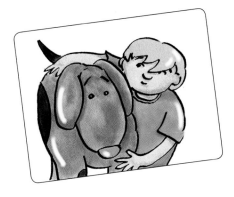

Homework

Exercise 1

Fill in the blanks below and write the answers in the puzzle.

Example

1 Alan is Julie's father. Julie is Mark's wife. Alan is Mark's __father-in-law__ .

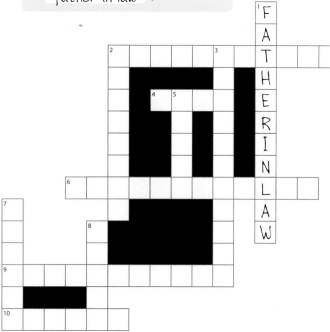

Across

2 Frank is Michael's father. Laura is Frank's mother. Laura is Michael's _____ .
4 Allison is Susan's mother. Carol is Allison's sister. Carol is Susan's _____ .
6 Melissa is Peter's wife. Jim is Melissa's brother. Peter is Jim's _____ .
9 Nick is Sam's brother. Patricia is Nick's wife. Patricia is Sam's _____ .
10 John is Billy's uncle. Susan is John's wife. Billy is Susan's _____ .

Down

2 Russell is Diane's son. George is Diane's father. Russell is George's _____ .
3 Jean is Nancy's daughter. Jack is Jean's husband. Nancy is Jack's _____ .
5 Jeff is Mary's husband. Mary is Ronnie's aunt. Jeff is Ronnie's _____ .
7 Bruce is Rita's son. Charlie is Rita's nephew. Bruce is Charlie's _____ .
8 Roger is Sally's father. Martin is Roger's brother. Sally is Martin's _____ .

Exercise 2

Write three sentences about your family members and leave one blank as in the sentences in Exercise 1.

Homework review

Work in groups of three to four students and compare your answers in the puzzle in Exercise 1.

Then read your three lines from Exercise 2 to the group. Repeat the lines until someone guesses the correct answer for the "blank."

Language focus

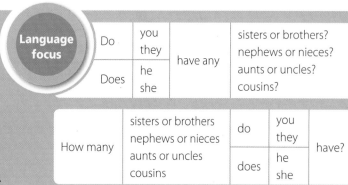

Review exercises

Exercise 1

The teacher will give you one of the pictures (1–4) below. There is a question for each picture. Write an answer for the question.

1

Man   Excuse me, how can we get to the pool?

2

Soldier   What does he look like?

3

Man   Do you have any children?

4

Delivery man   Where does it go?

Exercise 2

Read your answer to the class. Do not read the question. The class will guess your picture.

Listening task

Exercise 1 💿 55–59

Listen to the conversations (1–5) with your *book closed*. Then open your book and write the number of each conversation next to the correct picture.

Memo

- You can take notes as you listen.
- There is no conversation for one picture.

Exercise 2 💿 55–59

Listen again and write the *keywords* next to each picture.

Memo

Keywords are important words that tell you which picture to choose.

Student B, turn to page 102

Student A

Speaking task one

Exercise 1

The three pictures below are a little different from Student B's pictures. Ask and answer questions about the pictures and circle the differences.

Example	
Student A	Where's the dog?
Student B	It's under the umbrella, behind the woman.
Student A	That's different!

Memo

Sit face to face and do not look at your partner's pictures!

Exercise 2 Do this exercise with a partner.

Student A
Choose one of the figures below. This is you. Student B will ask questions to find out who you are.

Student B
Student A is one of the figures below. Ask Student A questions to find out which one he or she is.

Memo
- Don't use names in your *questions*, only when you guess.
- Don't ask about parents.
- Change roles and do the exercise again.

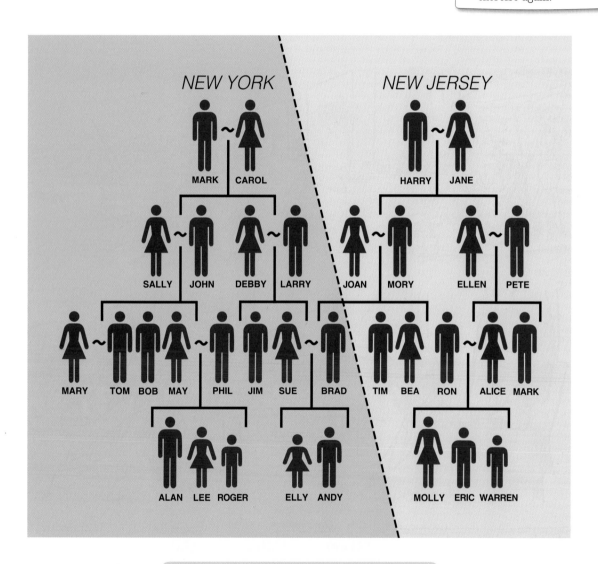

QUESTIONS
- Where do you live?
- Are you married?
- Do you have any brothers or sisters?
- How many brothers and sisters do you have?
- Do you have any children?
- How many children do you have?
- Is your son/daughter/brother/sister married?
- Do you have an older brother/sister?

Speaking task two   Do this exercise with everyone.

The teacher will give you one of the buildings (1–16) below. You live here.
Walk around the classroom and ask for and give directions. Find out where
other people live and write their names in the blanks below the map.

Example

Student A	Which station do you live near?
Student B	I live near Parkside Station.
Student A	How can I get to your apartment from the station?
Student B	Go straight for two blocks, turn right and it's on the right. It's just past the coffee shop, across from the park.

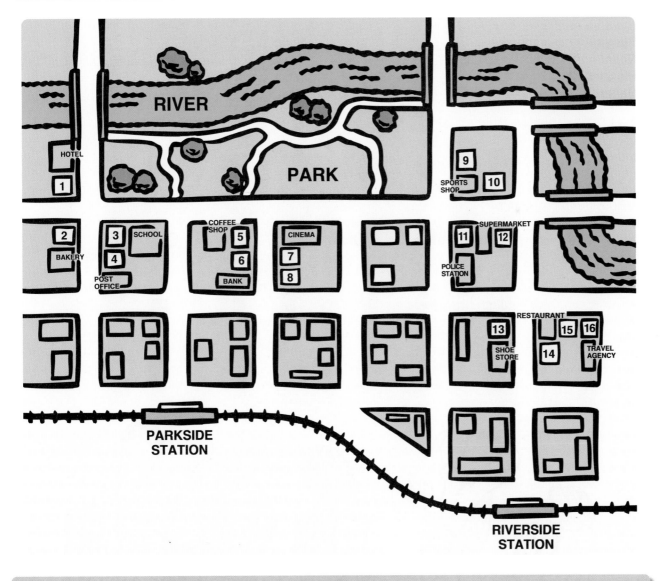

1		2		3		4	
5		6		7		8	
9		10		11		12	
13		14		15		16	

Caller, turn to page 103

Playe

Language game   Play this game with two to four "players" and one "caller."

Take turns choosing two numbers (1–24) from the grid below. Each number is a question or an answer. The caller will read each sentence that you choose.

Choose one number, listen to the caller read the sentence and then choose another number. Try to match a question with the answer. Do not write any notes. Just listen!

Continue until all the questions and answers have been matched. The player with the most matches wins!

> **Memo**
> - Cross off (✗) all matched numbers and circle *your* matches.
> - Look at this page only!
> - The teacher may let you write notes on the numbers.

Example

Player A	Number 8.	**Player B**	Number 7.
Caller	"What's he wearing?"	**Caller**	"He's wearing a jacket and tie."
Player A	Number 19.	**Player B**	Number 8.
Caller	"He's ninety-seven." They don't match!	**Caller**	"What's he wearing?" They match!

① ② ③ ④ ⑤ ⑥

⑦ ⑧ ⑨ ⑩ ⑪ ⑫

⑬ ⑭ ⑮ ⑯ ⑰ ⑱

⑲ ⑳ ㉑ ㉒ ㉓ ㉔

Warm-up exercises

Exercise 1

Write the man's answer.

Exercise 2 60

Listen to the following conversation. Then practice it with a partner.

Memo

Always look at the person you are speaking to. Don't look down at the page!

Grandfather	They have fish. Do you want fish?
Grandson	No, I don't like fish.
Grandfather	Oh. Well, how do you like roast beef?
Grandson	It's awful. I can't stand it.
Grandfather	OK. Do you like hamburgers?
Grandson	Hamburgers? I love hamburgers!

Exercise 3

Practice the conversation a few more times. Each time, use the ideas below or your own ideas.

spaghetti   chicken   pizza   chocolate cake   apple pie   ice cream

Look at page 65
Language focus

Listening task

Exercise 1 61

Listen to the conversation and write numbers (1–10) on the pictures as they are mentioned.

Exercise 2 61

Listen again and check (✓) the correct box in the chart for each one.

Exercise 3 61

Listen once more and write the keywords in the last column for each one.

	loves	likes	likes a little	dislikes	hates	keywords
1	☐	☐	☐	☐	☐	
2	☐	☐	☐	☐	☐	
3	☐	☐	☐	☐	☐	
4	☐	☐	☐	☐	☐	
5	☐	☐	☐	☐	☐	
6	☐	☐	☐	☐	☐	
7	☐	☐	☐	☐	☐	
8	☐	☐	☐	☐	☐	
9	☐	☐	☐	☐	☐	
10	☐	☐	☐	☐	☐	

Speaking task one   Do Exercise 1 alone and Exercise 2 with a partner.

Exercise 1

Write down one thing you love, one thing you like and one thing you hate for each subject.

	Food	Music	Leisure activities	Sports	Animals	TV shows
I love ...						
I like ...						
I hate ...						

Exercise 2

Ask your partner about the things on your list above. Write each thing in the correct place on the chart below, according to your partner's answer.

Memo

Rewrite the *things* from Exercise 1 on the chart. Do *not* make checks (✓) on the chart.

	Food	Music	Leisure activities	Sports	Animals	TV shows
Your partner loves ...						
Your partner likes ...						
Your partner likes ... a little.						
Your partner doesn't like ...						
Your partner hates ...						

Speaking task two   Do this exercise with everyone.

The teacher will give you one of the boxes below. Write your own idea in the blank on the bottom line. Walk around the classroom and ask yes/no questions or *Wh-* questions. Write the name of a different person in each blank.

Example

Student A	Do you like dancing?	Student B	How do you like pizza?
Student B	Not very much.	Student C	I love it!

1   Find someone who:

- loves pizza.
- likes snakes.
- doesn't like exercising.
- hates going shopping.

2   Find someone who:

- loves going to the movies.
- likes watching ice-skating.
- doesn't like coffee.
- hates snow.

3   Find someone who:

- loves rock and roll music.
- likes tea.
- doesn't like singing.
- hates cats.

4   Find someone who:

- loves going swimming.
- likes dancing.
- doesn't like hot weather.
- hates cooking.

5   Find someone who:

- loves chocolate.
- likes cold weather.
- dislikes Italian food.
- hates going to the beach.

6   Find someone who:

- loves reading.
- likes rainy days.
- doesn't like surprise parties.
- hates carrots.

7   Find someone who:

- loves Chinese food.
- likes writing letters.
- doesn't like baseball.
- hates going fishing.

8   Find someone who:

- loves cooking.
- likes going to the park.
- doesn't like small dogs.
- hates traveling by plane.

Homework

For each picture (1–7), write one question and one answer about likes and dislikes. (Write about anything for number 7.)

Example

1 Do you like watching TV?
I love it.

1

2

3

4

5

6

7

your own idea

Homework review   **Do this exercise with everyone.**

Walk around and talk to your classmates. Ask and answer questions about the six pictures above. For each one, find someone who wrote the same answer as you and write that person's name next to your sentence. Then ask your classmates about your own idea (number 7).

Language focus

.Do you like	baseball?
How do you like	cats?
	skiing?
	playing golf?

I love	it. / them.		It's / They're	great! / fantastic!		I'm crazy about	it. / them.
I like	it / them	a lot.					
I like	it. / them.						
I like	it / them	a little.	It's / They're	not bad. / OK.			
I don't like it / Not	very much.						
I don't like	it. / them.						
I hate	it. / them.		It's / They're	terrible! / awful!		I can't stand	it. / them.

65

12 ABOUT TOMORROW
The future

Warm-up exercises

Exercise 1

Write her boyfriend's answer.

Why can't you see me tomorrow? What are you going to do?

Exercise 2
 62

Listen to the following conversation. Then practice it with a partner.

Memo

Always look at the person you are speaking to. Don't look down at the page!

Yumi	Where are you going to go on your vacation?
Tim	I'm going to take a trip overseas, I think. Maybe I'll go scuba diving in Hawaii or skiing in France.
Yumi	That sounds expensive.
Tim	Expensive?
Yumi	Yeah, it's going to cost a fortune.
Tim	Really? Oh. Maybe I'll just go to the beach.

Exercise 3

Practice the conversation a few more times. Each time, use the ideas below or your own ideas.

Switzerland   London   Greece   Canada

Look at page 70

Language foc

Listening task

Exercise 1 · 63–65

Listen to the three conversations and write a number at the top of each of the small pictures to show the order they are mentioned (1–11).

Exercise 2 · 63–65

Listen again and write a note about Bobby's plans below each picture.

Example

buy a house

Student B, turn to page 104

Speaking task one

Listen to Student B and answer questions about what the people below are going to do. (Pictures in blue are tentative plans, or what they *may* do.) If you have blanks, ask Student B about what they are going to do and fill in the blanks.

> **Memo**
> - Write only *notes* in the blanks.
> - If the picture is in blue, answer, "He thinks he'll ... " or "Maybe he'll ... "

Example	
Student B	What's Wayne going to do in the morning?
Student A	He's going to take a shower and have breakfast. Then maybe he'll paint.

Wayne

Ellen

Hiroshi

Tom and Jane

Michelle

Student B

68

Speaking task two
Do this exercise in a group of three or more students.

The first student must choose a picture and say what he or she is going to do or may do this weekend. The next student must repeat the sentence and make one more sentence using a different picture. Each student must repeat every sentence and make one more sentence.

Continue around the circle and use as many pictures as possible, repeating all the sentences (with names) for about fifteen minutes (until your teacher says "stop").

The group of students that uses the most pictures, and correctly repeats the most sentences, wins!

Example

 Lenny   I'm going to get a haircut.

  Mary   Lenny's going to get a haircut. Maybe I'll go to the beach.

   Jean   Lenny's going to get a haircut. Maybe Mary will go to the beach. I think I'll wash my car.

    Lenny   I'm going to get a haircut. Maybe Mary will go to the beach. Jean thinks she'll wash her car. I'm going to go fishing.
               (continue)

12

Homework

You are going to have a one-week vacation from school. Choose *three* of the places below and write two or three things that you are going to do or may do at each place.

Memo

Write the sentences on a separate sheet of paper.

Example

- I am going to …
- Maybe I will …
- I think I will …

the park

a friend's house

the beach

the mall

the city

Homework review   Do this exercise with everyone.

Walk around and talk to your classmates. Find someone who is going to go to one of the same places as you. Then take turns asking and answering questions and find out how many of your plans are the same. Do the same for your other two places.

Memo

- Do this exercise in the next lesson if you have time.
- If you cannot find anyone, write "no one."

Language focus

Are	you / they	going to	do laundry?
Is	he / she		go to the library?
			go swimming?

Yes,	I	am.	No,	I'm	not.
	he / she	is.		he's / she's	
	we / they	are.		we're / they're	

What	are	you / they	going to do	tonight?
				tomorrow?
	is	he / she		on Sunday?
				next week?

I'm	going to	study.
They're		play tennis.
He's		go to the park.
She's		go fishing.

I	think	I'll	watch TV.
They		they'll	play golf.
He	thinks	he'll	go to the beach.
She		she'll	go bowling.

Maybe	I'll	read a book.
	they'll	play badminton.
	he'll	go to the movies.
	she'll	go skiing.

When	are	you / they	going to	go?
Where				
How	is	he / she		
Who				go with?

I'm	going to	go	on Friday.
They're			to Seaside Park.
He's			by car.
She's			with friends.

13 ABOUT YESTERDAY
The past

Warm-up exercises

Exercise 1

Write her boyfriend's answer.

So, what did you do yesterday?

Exercise 2 🔘 66

Listen to the following conversation. Then practice it with a partner.

> **Memo**
>
> Always look at the person you are speaking to. Don't look down at the page!

Dick	Where were you Friday night?
Jane	I was at home.
Dick	No, you weren't. Where did you go?
Jane	Oh, now I remember! I went to see a movie with Tina and Sue.
Dick	But they went shopping Friday evening!
Jane	We went shopping first and *then* went to see a movie.

Exercise 3

Practice the conversation a few more times. Each time, use the ideas below or your own ideas.

Look at page 75
Language focus

Listening task

Exercise 1 67

Listen to the conversation. Write "A" on the things Adam did and "B" on the things Brian did.

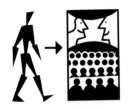   

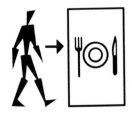   

Exercise 2 67

Listen again and write what Adam or Brian did below each picture.

Example

He went skiing.

72

Speaking task one   Do these exercises in groups of three or more students.

Exercise 1

Student A
Write "Y" for "yes" next to any twelve
pictures and write "N" for "no" next
to the other twelve pictures.

Students B and C
Choose sixteen of the activities and
write the numbers in random order in
your chart.

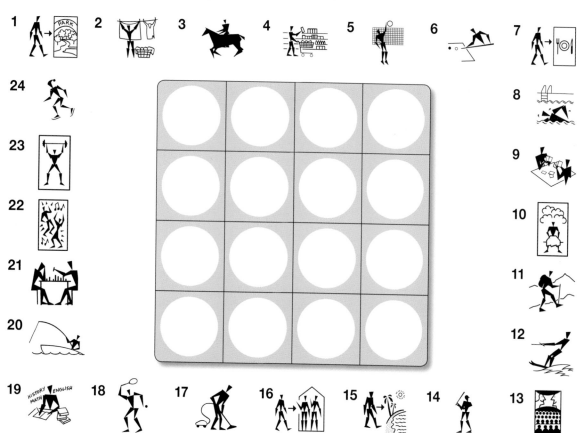

Exercise 2

Students B and C
Take turns and ask Student A about
the things in your chart. Circle (O)
numbers whenever Student A answers
"yes" and cross off (✗) numbers
whenever Student B answers "no."

Student A
Answer questions, "yes" (Y) or "no" (N):
• Answer "yes" and say which day
it was.
• Answer "no" in a full sentence.

Continue until all the numbers are marked. Each time you get four "Os" or "✗s" in a line, shout "Bingo!"
The student with the most "bingos" wins!

Example

| Student B | Did you go swimming last week? | Student C | Were you at the park last week? |
| Student A | Yes, I went swimming on Friday. | Student A | No, I wasn't at the park. |

Speaking task two
Do Exercise 1 alone and Exercise 2 with everyone.

Exercise 1

Write what you did last weekend. Include the place and as much information as you can for each time of day.

SATURDAY

morning

afternoon

evening

SUNDAY

morning

afternoon

evening

Exercise 2

Walk around the classroom and talk to your classmates about last weekend. For each time of day below (Saturday morning, Saturday afternoon, etc.), talk to a different classmate and write down what he or she did. Ask *Wh-* questions, such as, *what*, *who*, *where* and *when*, and write down as much information as you can.

Example

Student A	What did you do Saturday afternoon?	Student C	Where were you Sunday morning?
Student B	I went to the park.	Student D	I was at the mall.
Student A	Oh, yeah? Who did you go with?	Student C	Really? What did you do there?
Student B	I went with Sue.	Student D	I went clothes shopping.
Student A	How was it?	Student C	What did you buy?

SATURDAY

morning

afternoon

evening

SUNDAY

morning

afternoon

evening

13

Homework

Look at the two pictures of the house and write six or more sentences about the things that the family did.

Memo

Write the sentences on a separate sheet of paper.

Example

- They cleaned the table.
- They fixed the window.

Homework review   Do this exercise with everyone.

Walk around and talk to your classmates about the things that the family did. For each of the things you wrote about, find someone who wrote the same sentence as you and write that person's name next to your sentence.

Memo

- Do this exercise in the next lesson if you have time.
- If you cannot find anyone, write "no one."

Language focus

| Where | were | you / they | last night? | → | I / He / She | was | at home. |
| | was | he / she | on Sunday? | | We / They | were | in the library. |

| Were | you / we / they | late? | → | Yes, | I / he / she | was. | No, | I / he / she | wasn't. |
| Was | he / she | in class? | | | we / they | were. | | you / we / they | weren't. |

| What did | you / they | do | yesterday? | → | I / He / She | played tennis. |
| | he / she | | last week? | | We / They | went shopping. |

| Where | did | you / they | play tennis? | → | I / He / She | played tennis | in the park. |
| When | | he / she | go shopping? | | We / They | went shopping | on Sunday. |

| Did | you / they | go to the library? | → | Yes, | I / he / she | did. |
| | he / she | .do the homework? | | No, | we / they | didn't. |

Warm-up exercises

Look at page 80 Language foc

Exercise 1

Write the man's order.

Exercise 2 | 68

Listen to the following conversation. Then practice it with a partner.

Memo

Always look at the person you are speaking to. Don't look down at the page!

Waitress	May I help you?
Customer	I'd like a hamburger and fries.
Waitress	What would you like to drink?
Customer	I'll have a Coke.
Waitress	Small, medium or large?
Customer	Large, please.
Waitress	Anything else?
Customer	No, thank you.

Exercise 3

Practice the conversation a few more times. Each time, order something different from the menu.

🌿 MENU 🌿

Hamburger	Green Salad	
Cheeseburger	Tuna Salad	Dressing: Russian, French, Italian, Thousand Island
Steak	Mixed Salad	

Side Orders	Soft Drinks (Small/Medium/Large)	Dessert
French Fries	Coke	Ice Cream
Onion Rings	Pepsi	Cake
Baked Potato	7-Up	Pie

Listening task

Exercise 1 69

Listen to the conversation with your *book closed*. Then open your book and check (✓) all the questions that the waiter asked.

☐ May I help you?

☐ Are you ready to order?

☐ What would you like?

☐ Rare, medium or well-done?

☐ How would you like it?

☐ What kind of dressing would you like?

☐ Would you care for anything to drink?

☐ What would you like to drink?

☐ Large or small?

☐ Is that all?

☐ Anything else?

☐ Would you like your drinks now?

Exercise 2 69

Listen to the conversation again. Write "M" next to the things the man orders and "W" next to the things the woman orders.

MENU

BURGERS

Hamburger with tomato and onions	5.50

JUMBO BURGER 6.50
Quarter-pound burger
with tomato and onions

CHEESEBURGER 6.00
with melted cheese and onions

BACONBURGER 6.75
with bacon, lettuce and tomato

CHILIBURGER 6.75
Quarter-pound cheeseburger
with hot chili

SIDE ORDERS

Baked Potato	2.25
French Fries	2.50
Onion Rings	2.75
Salad	2.25

(Dressing: French/Italian/Russian)

DRINKS

Coke	1.95/2.35
7-Up	1.95/2.35
Root Beer	1.95/2.35
Milk Shake	2.95

(Vanilla/Chocolate/Strawberry)

Orange Juice	2.50
Coffee	1.75
Tea	1.75

Speaking task one   Do Exercise 1 alone and Exercise 2 with everyone.

Exercise 1

Look at the menu on page 79. Fill in the waiter's/waitress's question or the customer's order in each dialogue (1–9).

1
What would you like to drink?

A cup or a pot?

2
I'd like roast beef, please.

Well-done.

3
What kind of ice cream would you like?

Would you like a dish or a cone?

4
Could I have a green salad, please?

Italian.

5
Would you care for anything to drink?

Small, medium or large?

6
I'll have ice cream.

I'd like chocolate, please.

7
Could I have a Coke, please?

Large, please.

8
Excuse me, waiter!

I'd like a hamburger, please.

9
How would you like it?

And what kind of potato would you like?

Exercise 2

Walk around and read through the dialogues with your classmates. For each dialogue (1–9), find someone who wrote *exactly* the same sentence as you and write that person's name next to the waiter/waitress or customer.

> **Memo**
> • Speak to *one person* at a time.
> • Say the lines. Don't say the numbers!

Speaking task two   Do this exercise in a group of three students.

MENU

entrées

Prime Rib
Choice cuts of
prime beef

Sirloin Steak
Thick strip of
tender sirloin

Roast Beef
Juicy slices of
tender beef

Hamburger
100% pure beef
patty

All entrées come with your choice of
Potato (fries, baked or mashed) and
Vegetable (green peas, carrots or corn)

soup

French Onion Soup
Tomato Soup
Mushroom Soup

salad

Green Salad
Chef's Salad

Dressing: French, Italian,
Russian, Chinese

beverages

Soft Drinks -small
Coke   -medium
7-Up   -large
Root Beer
Sprite

Coffee & Tea
Coffee (cup or pot)
Tea (cup or pot)
Iced Tea
Café au lait
Cappuccino
(large or small)

dessert

Cake
Cheesecake, Fruitcake
Layer Cake

Pie
Apple Pie,
Banana Cream Pie,
Boston Cream Pie

Ice Cream (dish or cone)
Vanilla, Chocolate, Peach

Student A
You are a waiter or waitress. Take
Student B and Student C's order
and write it on the order pad below.

ORDER

Students B and C
You are restaurant customers.
Choose what you like from the menu
and give your order to Student A.

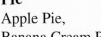

Memo
Do this exercise three times.
Take turns as Student A.

14

Homework

Write the lines of this dialogue in order and begin each line with "Waitress" or "Customer." ("Waitress" lines are in blue boxes.) Line numbers 5, 10, 15 and 20 have been marked.

Memo

Write the dialogue on a separate sheet of paper.

Medium.

No, thank you.

I'll have a Diet Coke.

Fine. Would you like something to drink?

How would you like it?

What kinds of soup do you have?

10 French onion soup sounds good. I'll have that.

Yes, we have Diet Coke, Diet Pepsi and Diet 7-Up.

Fine. Anything else?

Are you ready to order?

Baked, please.

20 Later, thank you.

Would you like soup or salad?

Yes, I'd like roast beef, please.

We have French onion soup, clam chowder and ...

Would you like your Coke now or later?

Large.

15 Large or small?

Do you have diet soda?

5 And what kind of potato would you like with that?

Homework review

Practice the dialogue with a partner and make sure all your lines are in the correct order.

Memo

• Do this exercise in the next lesson if you have time.

• Always look at your partner when you are speaking.

Language focus

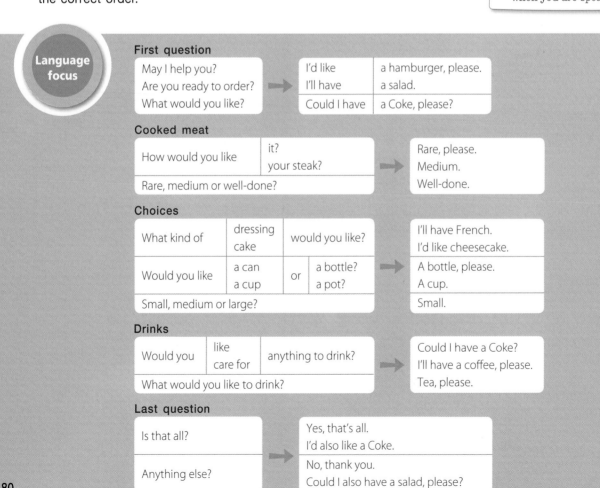

First question

May I help you?	I'd like	a hamburger, please.
Are you ready to order?	I'll have	a salad.
What would you like?	Could I have	a Coke, please?

Cooked meat

How would you like	it?	Rare, please.
	your steak?	Medium.
Rare, medium or well-done?		Well-done.

Choices

What kind of	dressing cake	would you like?	I'll have French. I'd like cheesecake.
Would you like	a can a cup	or	a bottle? a pot?	A bottle, please. A cup.
Small, medium or large?			Small.

Drinks

| Would you | like care for | anything to drink? | Could I have a Coke? I'll have a coffee, please. |
| What would you like to drink? | | | Tea, please. |

Last question

| Is that all? | Yes, that's all. I'd also like a Coke. |
| Anything else? | No, thank you. Could I also have a salad, please? |

Review exercises

Exercise 1

The teacher will give you one of the pictures (1–4) below. There is a question for each picture. Write an answer for the question.

Memo

- Write on a separate sheet of paper.
- If you finish early, write an answer for *another* picture.

1

Waitress   Are you ready to order?

2

Man   By yourself? What are you going to do?

3

Man   So, how do you like horseback riding?

4

Cook   Why didn't you eat your sandwich?

Exercise 2

Read your answer to the class. Do *not* read the question. The class will guess your picture.

Memo

Try to memorize your answer for Exercise 2.

Listening task

Exercise 1 70–74

Listen to the conversations (1–5) with your *book closed*. Then open your book
and write the number of each conversation next to the correct picture.

Exercise 2 70–74

Listen again and write the *keywords* next to each picture.

Speaking task one

Exercise 1

Give Student B clues for each answer in Crossword puzzle 1 until Student B guesses the answer. Use "blanks" in your clues. (You can give more than one clue for an answer.)

Memo

For help with clues, you can look at the unit shown for each word, but try to make up your own sentences.

Example

Student B	What's 1 down?
Student A	I can't drive a car, but I can ride a "blank."
Student B	A motorcycle?
Student A	That's right!

Crossword puzzle 1

Unit 1: Abilities
Unit 2: Personal information
Unit 2: Personal information
Unit 3: Time and date
Unit 3: Time and date

Unit 14: In a restaurant

Unit 7: Directions

Unit 3: Time and date

Unit 6: Location and moving things

Unit 7: Directions

Exercise 2

Ask Student B for clues and fill in Crossword puzzle 2. In each clue, the "blank" in Student B's sentence is the answer.

Example

Student A	What's 2 across?
Student B	I love it! It's great! It's "blank!"
Student A	Fantastic?
Student B	That's right!

Crossword puzzle 2

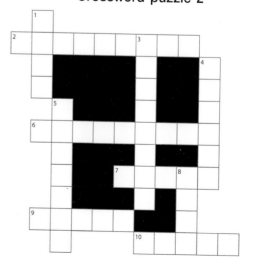

Speaking task two   Do this exercise with everyone.

The teacher will give you one of the boxes on pages 84 and 85. Walk around the classroom and ask yes/no questions. Write the name of a different person in each blank.

Also ask each classmate a *Wh-* question, such as, *who, what, when, where* and *why* for extra information. Write the extra information in the blank below the name.

Example

Student A	Did you go to the movies last week?	**Student A**	Are you going overseas next summer?
Student B	Yes, I did.	**Student C**	Yes, I am.
Student A	What movie did you see?	**Student A**	Where are you going to go?
Student B	I saw *Harry Potter*.	**Student C**	I'm going to go to Korea.

---

1   Find someone who:

_____ went to the movies last week.
name

_____
extra information

_____ is going to go overseas next summer.
name

_____
extra information

_____ usually reads in bed at night.
name

_____
extra information

---

2   Find someone who:

_____ went shopping yesterday.
name

_____
extra information

_____ is going to go to the movies this week.
name

_____
extra information

_____ watches TV every day.
name

_____
extra information

---

3   Find someone who:

_____ went to a party last month.
name

_____
extra information

_____ is going to go shopping this weekend.
name

_____
extra information

_____ usually eats lunch at school.
name

_____
extra information

---

4   Find someone who:

_____ watched sports on TV last night.
name

_____
extra information

_____ is going to go out with friends tonight.
name

_____
extra information

_____ often goes to the movies.
name

_____
extra information

Memo

- Give true answers.
- Change partners often.
- If you cannot find anyone, write "no one."

Example

Student B	Do you go overseas every year?	Student B	Are you going to call someone today?
Student C	Yes, I do.	Student D	Yes, I am.
Student B	Where do you go?	Student B	Who are you going to call?
Student C	I go to China to visit my family.	Student D	I'm going to call my cousin.

5 Find someone who:

_____ ate in a restaurant last weekend.
name

_____
extra information

_____ is going to call someone today.
name

_____
extra information

_____ goes overseas every year.
name

_____
extra information

6 Find someone who:

_____ went out of town last summer.
name

_____
extra information

_____ is going to eat out tonight.
name

_____
extra information

_____ often calls overseas.
name

_____
extra information

7 Find someone who:

_____ listened to the radio today.
name

_____
extra information

_____ is going to go shopping today.
name

_____
extra information

_____ sometimes writes letters.
name

_____
extra information

8 Find someone who:

_____ called someone today.
name

_____
extra information

_____ is going to cook tonight.
name

_____
extra information

_____ usually walks to school.
name

_____
extra information

Caller, turn to page 106

Player

Language game   Play this game with two to four "players" and one "caller."

Take turns choosing two numbers (1–24) from the grid below. Each number is a question or an answer. The caller will read each sentence that you choose.

Choose one number, listen to the caller read the sentence and then choose another number. Try to match a question with the answer. Do not write any notes. Just listen!

Continue until all the questions and answers have been matched. The player with the most matches wins!

> **Memo**
> * Cross off (✗) all matched numbers and circle *your* matches.
> * Look at this page only!
> * The teacher may let you write notes on the numbers.

Example

Player A	Number 12.	Player B	Number 15.
Caller	"Medium, please."	Caller	"How would you like your steak?"
Player A	Number 3.	Player B	Number 12.
Caller	"Yes it is!" They don't match!	Caller	"Medium, please." They match!

1   2   3   4   5   6

7   8   9   10   11   12

13   14   15   16   17   18

19   20   21   22   23   24

APPENDIX

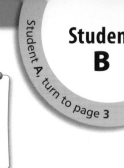

Speaking task one

Listen to Student A and answer the questions. If you have blanks, ask Student A questions and fill in the blanks.

Memo

• For spelling ask, "How do you spell that?"

• In box 4 you can use your hometown to answer the question "Where are you from?"

1

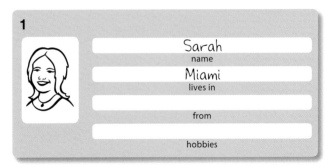

Sarah
name

Miami
lives in

from

hobbies

2

name

Australia
live in

from

hiking and fishing
hobbies

3

name

lives in

Los Angeles
from

water skiing
hobbies

4

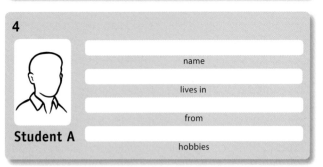

name

lives in

from

Student A

hobbies

Student A, turn to page 7

Speaking task one

Take turns asking and answering questions with Student A. If you have blanks, ask Student A questions and fill in the blanks. Listen to Student A and answer the questions.

Example			
Student A	Does Mary know how to sing?	**Student B**	Can she play the piano?
Student B	Yes, she does.	**Student A**	Uh-uh.

Memo

Ask and answer in *different* ways, but only write "yes," "no" or "a little" in the blanks.

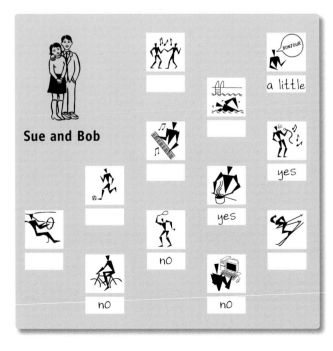

Student A, turn to page 13

Speaking task one

Take turns with Student A asking and answering questions. Ask Student A for information to fill in the blanks in the chart.

Example

Student B	Where's Cathy from?
Student A	She's from the United States.

Memo

Answer in full sentences, but only write *notes* in your blanks.

Name	 Cathy	 Bill	 Lee	 Yoon-Hee	 Mike and Lily	 Student A
Where / from?		Australia		Korea		
Which part?		Sydney		Busan		
Age?		30		25		
Married?		yes		no		
Children?		two boys		no		
Occupation?		a student		an office worker		
WORK — Who / for?				British Embassy		
WORK — Where / work?				Seoul		
STUDY — What / studying?		Business				
STUDY — School?		University of Arizona				

90

Speaking task one

Exercise 1

Ask Student A the time and draw the hands on each clock (1–12).

Example

Student B	Excuse me, what time is it?
Student A	It's a quarter after seven.

Memo

Use different ways to ask and tell the time.

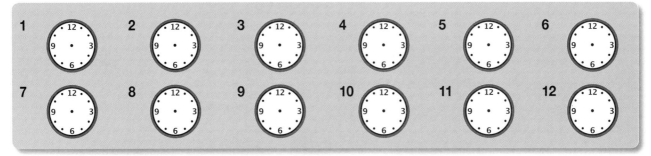

Vocabulary

- exactly
- on the dot
- past
- after
- to
- before
- a quarter
- half past

Exercise 2

Look at each clock (1–12) and tell Student A the time.

Example

Student A	Pardon me, do you know the time?
Student B	It's half past twelve.

Exercise 3 Do this exercise with a partner.

Ask Student B for the birthdays of the people below and fill in the blanks under "Birthday." Tell Student A the birthdays of the people below. Then write every name under the correct zodiac sign in the chart on the right.

Memo

Use different ways to ask and tell the date.

Example		
Student B When's Mary's birthday?	**Student A** What date's Jane's birthday?
Student A It's December the twenty-seventh.	**Student B** It's the fifteenth of February.

Name	Birthday
Mary	
Jane	2/15
Mike	3/31
Helen	9/30
Marty	
Alan	11/7
Ronnie	
John	12/2
Milly	
Mark	
Ellen	2/23
Loni	

Capricorn
December 22 – January19

name

name

Aquarius
January 20 – February 18

name

name

Pisces
February 19 – March 20

name

name

Aries
March 21 – April 19

name

name

Taurus
April 20 – May 20

name

name

Gemini
May 21 – June 20

name

name

Cancer
June 21 – July 22

name

name

Leo
July 23 – August 22

name

name

Virgo
August 23 – September 22

name

name

Libra
September 23 – October 22

name

name

Scorpio
October 23 – November 21

name

name

Sagittarius
November 22 – December 21

name

name

Exercise 4 Do this exercise with everyone.

Walk around the classroom and ask your classmates for their birthdays. Find one person for each zodiac sign and write his or her name and birthday in the blank.

Speaking task two

Do this exercise with everyone.

The teacher will divide the class into two halves, Group A and Group B, and give each student in Group B some of the information boxes below. Answer Group A's questions, but answer only the questions that you have information to answer. For all other questions answer, "Sorry, I don't know."

Example

Student A	It's a quarter after twelve in New York. What time is it in London?
Student B	It's a quarter after five in London.
Student A	When's St. Patrick's Day in Ireland?
Student B	It's the seventeenth of March.

Memo

- Check (✓) the boxes the teacher gives you.
- *Group B* students may stay in their seats.

1 Canada Day in Canada is 7/1.

2 Australia Day in Australia is 1/26.

3 Children's Day in Japan is 5/5.

4 New York → London

5 Paris → London

6 Independence Day in Russia is 6/12.

7 Bastille Day in France is 7/14.

8 Paris → Sydney

9 St. Patrick's Day in Ireland is 3/17.

10 Independence Day in the United States is 7/4.

11 Boxing Day in the United Kingdom is 12/26.

12 New York → London

13 Republic Day in India is 1/26.

14 Constitution Day in Thailand is 12/10.

15 Constitution Memorial Day in Japan is 5/3.

16 Memorial Day in the United States is 5/30.

17 Seoul → Beijing

18 National Day in Singapore is 8/9.

19 Seoul → Bangkok

20 Tokyo → Rome

21 Thanksgiving Day in Canada is 10/9.

22 National Day in Switzerland is 8/9.

23 National Day in China is 10/1.

24 Tokyo → Quebec

Speaking task one

Take turns asking and answering questions with Student A. If you have blanks, ask Student A questions and fill in the blanks. Listen to Student A and answer the questions.

Example

Student B	What does Bob do?	Student A	Where does he have lunch?
Student A	He's a truck driver.	Student B	He has lunch at a coffee shop.

> **Memo**
> Answer in full sentences, but only write *notes* in your blanks.

Name / Occupation	🏠→🚶	🚶→🏢	🚶→🍽	🍽	🏠←🚶	🌙
Bob	(clock)	(clock)	at a coffee shop	with his friends	(clock)	
Ted salesperson	(clock)	(clock)			(clock)	🚶→🍽 / 📻🎵
Carol	(clock)	(clock)	in the company cafeteria	with her boss	(clock)	
Alice nurse	(clock)	(clock)	in the hospital cafeteria		(clock)	
Jack	(clock)	(clock)		with other drivers	(clock)	🚶→🏠 / 🖼
Betty waitress	(clock)	(clock)			(clock)	🖼 / 💻
Student A	(clock)	(clock)			(clock)	

QUESTIONS

- What does Bob do?
- What time does he leave home?
- What time does he get to work?
- Where does he have lunch?
- Who does he have lunch with?
- What time does he get home?
- What does he do in the evening?

94

⑤

Speaking task one
Play this game with one "caller" and two "players."

Choose one of the boxes (1–9) below and use the box to play Bingo. Listen to the caller.
Cross off (✗) any picture that the caller mentions. If you get three "✗s" in a line, shout "Bingo!"

Example	
	Caller I can play the piano a little.
	Caller She usually gets home at half past ten. (continue)

Memo
- Each player choose a different box to start.
- Play again: each student take a turn as the caller.

1

2

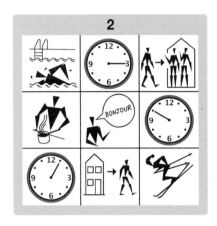

3

4

5

6

7

8

9

Player, turn to page 31

Language game   Play this game with two to four "players" and one "caller."

Before you begin the game, number the questions and answers below from 1 to 24 in random order (all mixed up).

The players will take turns choosing two numbers. Listen for the first number and read the first sentence. Listen for the second number, read the second sentence and say if it matches the first sentence or not.* After that, the next player chooses.

Continue until all the questions and answers have been matched. The player with the most matches wins!

*You can also ask the players if it is a match before you tell them.

> ### Memo
> - Read each sentence slowly, once or twice.
> - Read both of the sentences *before* you say, "They match!" or "They don't match!"

Example

Player A	Number 4.	Player B	Number 23.
Caller	"What does he do?"	Caller	"He's a photographer."
Player A	Number 11.	Player B	Number 4.
Caller	"No, he isn't." They don't match!	Caller	"What does he do?" They match!

Question	Answer
◯ What's she studying?	◯ She's studying fashion design.
◯ What school does she go to?	◯ She goes to the University of Milan.
◯ Does she have any children?	◯ No, she doesn't. She's single and a student.
◯ What does she usually do on Sunday?	◯ She does housework and goes shopping.
◯ Does she have any hobbies?	◯ Yes, her hobbies are skiing and photography.
◯ What does he do?	◯ He's a photographer.
◯ Does he know how to ski?	◯ Yes, he does. He goes skiing every winter.
◯ Is he married?	◯ No, he isn't.
◯ How old is he?	◯ Forty-five.
◯ When's his birthday?	◯ The thirtieth of March.
◯ Who do they work for?	◯ They work for *Fashion Magazine*.
◯ How many children do they have?	◯ Two, one boy and one girl.

Speaking task two

Some of the objects are in different places in Student A's picture. Take turns asking questions about location and telling each other where to move the objects to make the pictures the same. (Only move objects that are in different places.)

Example

Student A	Where's the broom?	Student B	Where are the skis?
Student B	It's on the floor, next to the workbench.	Student A	They're next to the side door, on the right.
Student A	That's the same.	Student B	That's different. Pick them up and put them ...

Memo

To move an object, cross it out and draw it in the new place.

Vocabulary

OBJECTS			LOCATIONS
• gas can	• golf clubs	• saw	• cabinet
• lawn mower	• paintbrushes	• tennis rackets	• garage door
• patio umbrella	• paint cans	• shovel	• side door
• ladder	• rake	• tires	• shelf
• lawn chairs	• hose	• toolbox	• workbench
• bicycles	• garbage cans	• screens	• corner

97

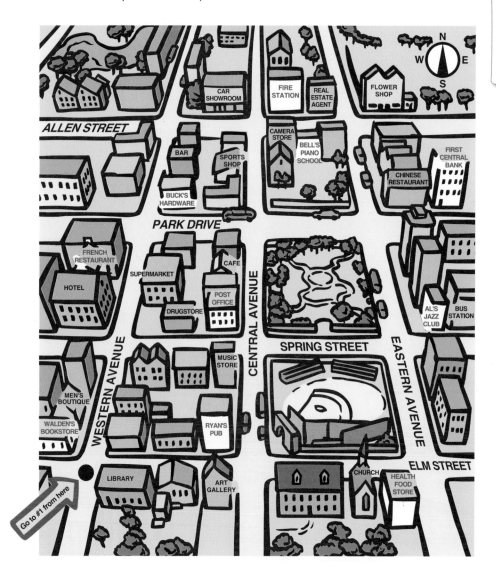

Student A, turn to page 41

Speaking task two

Exercise 1

Look at the map and give directions to Student A. (Student A does not know the names of the places in red.)

Memo

Go to each new place from the previous place: go to #2 from #1, then go to #3 from #2 and so on.

Exercise 2

Ask Student A for directions to each place below. Write the name of each place on the building.

PLACES

- Shelley's Dance School
- Tracy's Karate School
- the video rental store
- Adam's Health Club
- the police station
- the Skyline Diner
- the Mexican restaurant
- the Japanese restaurant
- the subway station
- Jake's Autoshop

Student A, turn to page 45

Student B

Speaking task one

Take turns asking and answering questions about the people (A–P) below. Ask about people you do not have names for. Fill in the blanks with the correct names.

Example

Student A	What's that woman's name?
Student B	Which woman?
Student A	She's tall, and she has curly black hair, and she's wearing a long dress.
Student B	Her name's Ruth.

> **Memo**
> • Ask only about appearance.
> • Sit face to face with your partner.

A		**B**	Carl	**C**		**D**	
E	Maria	**F**	Linda	**G**		**H**	Henry
I		**J**	Ruth	**K**		**L**	Mary
M		**N**	Robert	**O**	Julie	**P**	

Speaking task two

The men on the stage below are different from the men in Student A's picture. Take turns asking and answering yes/no questions about each man and circle the differences.

Example	
Student A	Is the first man wearing black shoes?
Student B	No, he isn't. He's wearing boots.
Student A	That's different!

> **Memo**
> - Only the six men on the stage are different.
> - Start with the man on the left.

Speaking task one

Exercise 1

Answer Student A's questions about "your family" on this page.
These are pictures of you and your brothers and sisters.

Ken

My older brother is married.
He is a doctor and lives in
Brighton. He is 28.

Peter

My younger brother is a
high school student. He is
15 and lives with my
parents in London.

Student B
Lee

June

Betty

I am an office worker,
and I live in Eastbourne.
I am 23 and married.

My older sister is married and
has two children. She lives in
Reading. She is 26.

My second oldest sister is a
software engineer and lives in
Oxford. She is 24 and still single.

Exercise 2

Ask Student A questions.
Write the answers on the
questionnaire.

1 Name:		2 Age:			
3 Occupation:		4 Married: Yes ☐ No ☐			
	Name	Age	Married	Occupation	Lives in
5 Brothers:					
6 Sisters:					

Exercise 3

Answer Student A's questions about yourself and your *actual*
brothers and sisters. (Just answer, do not write!)

> **Memo**
> If you or your partner have no
> brothers or sisters, talk about cousins.

Exercise 4

Ask Student A questions
about his or her *actual*
brothers and sisters.
Write the answers on the
questionnaire.

1 Name:		2 Age:			
3 Occupation:		4 Married: Yes ☐ No ☐			
	Name	Age	Married	Occupation	Lives in
5 Brothers:					
6 Sisters:					

Speaking task one

Exercise 1

The three pictures below are a little different from Student A's pictures. Ask and answer questions about the pictures and circle the differences.

Example

Student A	Where's the dog?
Student B	It's under the umbrella, behind the woman.
Student A	That's different!

Memo

Sit face to face and do not look at your partner's pictures!

Caller

Player, turn to page 60

Language game Play this game with two to four "players" and one "caller."

Before you begin the game, number the questions and answers below from 1 to 24 in random order (all mixed up).

The players will take turns choosing two numbers. Listen for the first number and read the first sentence. Listen for the second number, read the second sentence and say if it matches the first sentence or not.* After that, the next player chooses.

Continue until all the questions and answers have been matched. The player with the most matches wins!

*You can also ask the players if it is a match before you tell them.

Memo

- Read each sentence slowly, once or twice.
- Read both of the sentences *before* you say, "They match!" or "They don't match!"

Example

Player A	Number 8.		**Player B**	Number 7.
Caller	"What's he wearing?"		**Caller**	"He's wearing a jacket and tie."
Player A	Number 19.		**Player B**	Number 8.
Caller	"He's ninety-seven." They don't match!		**Caller**	"What's he wearing?" They match!

Question	Answer
◯ Excuse me, where's the hospital?	◯ It's straight ahead, just past the park.
◯ Are the restrooms on this floor?	◯ Uh huh, just past women's clothes.
◯ Where do the CDs go?	◯ They go in the bottom drawer of my desk.
◯ Where does the ice cream go?	◯ It goes in the freezer, on the top shelf.
◯ How old's your grandfather?	◯ He's ninety-seven.
◯ How many cousins do you have?	◯ Nine.
◯ Does your brother live in London?	◯ No, he doesn't. He lives in Rome.
◯ Who's that guy in the kitchen?	◯ My brother-in-law.
◯ Does your sister have any children?	◯ Yes, she does, one boy and two girls.
◯ What's he wearing?	◯ He's wearing a jacket and tie.
◯ Is John tall?	◯ Yes, he is, and he has long hair.
◯ What does Mary look like?	◯ She's short and thin.

Student A, turn to page 68

Student B

Speaking task one

Listen to Student A and answer questions about what the people below are going to do. (Pictures in blue are tentative plans, or what they *may* do.) If you have blanks, ask Student A about what they are going to do and fill in the blanks.

> **Memo**
> - Write only *notes* in the blanks.
> - If the picture is in blue, answer, "He thinks he'll ... " or "Maybe he'll ... "

Example

Student B	What's Wayne going to do in the morning?
Student A	He's going to take a shower and have breakfast. Then maybe he'll paint.

Wayne

Ellen

Hiroshi

Tom and Jane

Michelle

Student A

Student A, turn to page 83

Student B

Speaking task one

Exercise 1

Ask Student A for clues and fill in Crossword puzzle 1. In each clue, the "blank" in Student A's sentence is the answer.

Example

Student B	What's 1 down?
Student A	I can't drive a car, but I can ride a "blank."
Student B	A motorcycle?
Student A	That's right!

Crossword puzzle 1

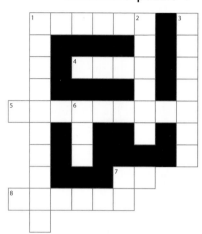

Exercise 2

Give Student A clues for each answer in Crossword puzzle 2 until Student A guesses the answer. Use "blanks" in your clues. (You can give more than one clue for an answer.)

Example

Student A	What's 2 across?
Student B	I love it! It's great! It's "blank!"
Student A	Fantastic?
Student B	That's right!

Memo

For help with clues, you can look at the unit shown for each word, but try to make up your own sentences.

Unit 8: Describing people
Unit 8: Describing people
Unit 12: The future
Unit 11: Likes and dislikes
Unit 13: The past

Crossword puzzle 2

Unit 11: Likes and dislikes

Unit 13: The past

Unit 14: In a restaurant

Unit 9: Talking about family

Unit 9: Talking about family

²FANTASTIC
¹T O ⁴P
L O L
L M A
⁵W O
⁶YESTERDAY
A R E
R ⁷WOUL⁸D
I W O
⁹UNCLE V
G ¹⁰NIECE

Language game   Play this game with two to four "players" and one "caller."

Before you begin the game, number the questions and answers below from 1 to 24 in random order (all mixed up).

The players will take turns choosing two numbers. Listen for the first number and read the first sentence. Listen for the second number, read the second sentence and say if it matches the first sentence or not.* After that, the next player chooses.

Continue until all the questions and answers have been matched. The player with the most matches wins!

*You can also ask the players if it is a match before you tell them.

> **Memo**
> - Read each sentence slowly, once or twice.
> - Read both of the sentences *before* you say, "They match!" or "They don't match!"

Example

Player A	Number 12.	Player B	Number 15.
Caller	"Medium, please."	Caller	"How would you like your steak?"
Player A	Number 3.	Player B	Number 12.
Caller	"Yes, it is!" They don't match!	Caller	"Medium, please." They match!

Question	Answer
( ) What are you going to do tonight?	( ) Maybe I'll go to the movies with Mary.
( ) When are we going to catch the bus?	( ) Around half past one.
( ) Are we going to eat out tonight?	( ) No, I think I'll cook steak for dinner. OK?
( ) Why wasn't Mary here this morning?	( ) She was late. She missed the bus.
( ) Did you go to the movies last night?	( ) No, we went bowling.
( ) What kind of ice cream would you like?	( ) I'll have vanilla.
( ) How would you like your steak?	( ) Medium, please.
( ) Would you like anything to drink?	( ) No, thank you.
( ) What did they have for lunch?	( ) They had spaghetti.
( ) How do you like ice cream?	( ) I love it!
( ) Do you like spiders?	( ) No! I can't stand them!
( ) Is this English course almost finished?	( ) Yes, it is!

 **Self-study exercises**

Exercise 1 1

Listen to the conversation and check (✓) the five questions that *can* be answered. Then listen again and write the answer.

☐ What subject can't Dick do?

☐ What is Dick's favorite subject?

☐ What does Dad think of the math problem?

☐ Where did Mom learn to play the piano?

☐ What two sports is Mom good at?

☐ What foreign language can Mom speak?

☐ Who knows how to play baseball?

☐ What does Mom like to cook?

Exercise 2 2

Rewrite these sentences from the conversation in the correct order. Then listen and check your answers.

> **Memo**
>
> Add punctuation and use capital letters where necessary.

1 Dad / do math / you can't / either

_____

2 good at / things / Mom's / a lot of

_____

3 the piano / Mom / play / how to / knows

_____

4 how to / right / you / cook / know

_____

 Self-study exercise

Listen to each conversation and put the lines in order.

Conversation one 3

	I'm a journalist.
	Where do you work?
	What do you do?
	With friends in New York.
	I work in London.
	I work for *City Life Magazine*.
	Where are you going to stay while you're here?
	Who do you work for?

Conversation two 4

	I go to UCLA. It's my first year.
	That's interesting. What school do you go to?
	Oh, really? What are you studying?
	Oh, yeah? How do you like it?
	Oh, it's great. But I'm failing French.
	I'm a student.
	I'm studying child psychology.
	So tell me, Susan, what do you do?

Conversation three 5

	Quebec.
	I'm a high school teacher.
	Where are you from, Miss Ames?
	I see. When do you plan to return home?
	Oh? Where in Canada?
	Oh, in about three weeks.
	Hmm ... and what do you do?
	I'm from Canada.

3 Self-study exercises

Exercise 1

Listen to the conversations (1–4). Find the differences in each conversation below.

Conversation one 6

Woman	Excuse me, what time does the mall open?
Man	It opens at eight forty.
Woman	And what time does it close today?
Man	It closes at ten past seven.

Conversation two 7

Woman	When do you leave for London?
Man	I leave on February nineteenth.
Woman	And when do you return?
Man	I return on March fifteenth.

Conversation three 8

Man	When's your father's birthday?
Woman	It's May twenty-third.
Man	And when's your sister's birthday?
Woman	Her birthday's October the second.

Conversation four 9

Man	Pardon me, when does this park open in the morning?
Woman	It opens at quarter past nine.
Man	And when does it close in the evening?
Woman	It closes at half past eight.

Exercise 2

Listen to the conversations (5–8). Fill in the missing words.

Conversation five 10

Man	What day does the course begin?
Woman	It begins _____ September the sixth.
Man	When does it end?
Woman	It ends _____ the twelfth _____ December.

Conversation six 11

Woman	Hello? Could you tell me what time breakfast _____
Man	Yes, it begins _____ half past seven, in the dining room.
Woman	And what time _____ lunch?
Man	Lunch _____ at a quarter to twelve.

Conversation seven 12

Man	_____ does the movie start?
Woman	It starts _____ twenty to five.
Man	Uh huh, and when does it finish?
Woman	It's _____ at ten past seven.

Conversation eight 13

Man	When does the beach open _____ the summer?
Woman	It opens May thirtieth.
Man	When does it close?
Woman	It closes _____ the first _____ September.

Self-study exercises

Exercise 1 14

Listen to the conversation and check (✓) the five questions that *can* be answered. Then listen again and write the answers to the five questions.

What does Chris think of married life?

Where did Chris meet his wife?

When does Chris see Mariko?

Who goes to work earlier?

What does Chris do?

What does Mariko do in the morning?

What time does Mariko eat dinner?

What time does Chris go to bed?

Exercise 2 15

Rewrite these sentences from the conversation in the correct order. Then listen and check your answers.

> **Memo**
> Add punctuation and use capital letters where necessary.

1   she / in the morning / go to work / does

_____

2   you / dinner / don't have / so / together

_____

3   reads / twenty past eleven / gets home / around / until midnight / and / she

_____

4   what / on weekends / do you two / usually / so / do

_____

110

 Self-study exercises

www.fifty-fifty-series.com

Exercise 1 16–23

Listen to the sentences. Find the differences.

Memo

Cross out (✗) the words that don't match and write in the correct words.

1 Pick up the magazines and put them in the desk.

2 Take the wine glasses and put them under the coffee table.

3 Pick up the DVD and put it on the TV.

4 Take the remote control and put it on the bookcase, between the lamp and the fireplace.

5 Pick up the photo album and place it on the coffee table.

6 Pick up the sunglasses and put them on the bed.

7 Pick up the pillow on the floor and put it on the sofa.

8 Take the chess set and put it beside the lamp on the bookcase, on the left.

Exercise 2 24–31

Listen to the sentences. Fill in the missing words.

Memo

Add punctuation and use capital letters where necessary.

1 The pillow's on the _____.

2 The _____ are on the desk.

3 The camera's on the _____.

4 The DVD's _____ the TV.

5 The wine _____ are on the desk.

6 The magazines are on the _____ table.

7 The _____ set's on the bookcase, next to the lamp.

8 The _____ album's between the lamp and the fireplace.

Self-study exercises

Listen to the conversations (1–5) and write "T" (true) or "F" (false) next to each sentence.

Conversation one 32

The man is looking for the hotel.

The hotel is far away.

Conversation two 33

The man should turn left at the second corner.

The doctor's office is in the middle of the block.

Conversation three 34

The man should turn right at the post office.

The saloon is across from the hotel.

Conversation four 35

The man is looking for the feed store.

The bank is just past the feed store.

Conversation five 36

The man wants to go to the sheriff's office.

The sheriff's office is just before the bank.

Exercise 2

Rewrite the false sentences to make them true.

112

8 Self-study exercise

 37

Listen to the conversation and choose the best answer to each question.

1 What is this conversation mainly about?

   a. Pam's boyfriend

   b. Pam's classmates

   c. Pam's sister

   d. Pam's teacher

2 Who is Pam's roommate?

   a. Andrea

   b. Deb

   c. Melanie

   d. Amy

3 What is Melanie like?

   a. popular

   b. funny

   c. lazy

   d. careless

4 Who is the class clown?

   a. Melanie

   b. Amy

   c. Rod

   d. Lee

5 What is Amy wearing?

   a. a plaid shirt

   b. a white, short-sleeved shirt

   c. a polka dot skirt and sneakers

   d. glasses and a vest

6 Amy and Lee are _____ .

   a. friends

   b. girlfriend and boyfriend

   c. sister and brother

   d. roommates

Self-study exercises

Exercise 1  38

Listen to the conversation and check (✓) the five questions that *can* be answered. Then listen again and write the answers to the five questions.

☐ Who is in the picture?

☐ Who took the picture?

☐ When did Jean go to her uncle's house?

☐ What does Jean's brother do?

☐ Who is Amy?

☐ How old is Pamela?

☐ What is the name of Jean's cousin?

☐ Where did Mary study art?

Exercise 2 39

Rewrite these sentences from the conversation in the correct order. Then listen and check your answers.

> **Memo**
>
> Add punctuation and use capital letters where necessary.

1   going to be / next month / he's / five

_____

2   your uncle / so / here / this is

_____

3   on the / Mary / left / his wife / that's

_____

4   this picture / the fireplace / she / over / painted

_____

114

Self-study exercises

Exercise 1 40

Listen to the conversation and check (✓) the five questions that *can* be answered. Then listen again and write the answers to the five questions.

Which state does Ken live in?	
Why doesn't Ken like the weather?	
Where does Ken come from?	
What American food does Ken not like?	
What does Ken think of American football?	
Which football team does Ken support?	
What kind of music does Ken like?	
What is Ken studying?	

Exercise 2 41

Rewrite these sentences from the conversation in the correct order. Then listen and check your answers.

> **Memo**
> Add punctuation and use capital letters where necessary.

1   I / mosquitoes / and / can't stand

_____

2   I'm / about / crazy / well / pizza

_____

3   TV / you / do / watching / like

_____

4   a little / they're / boring / sometimes / but / not bad

_____

 **Self-study exercise**

Listen to the three conversations and choose the best answer to each question.

Conversation one (Sister and Brother) 42

1 What is this conversation mainly about?

   a. Bobby's call from Las Vegas
   b. Bobby's new house in the mountains
   c. calling his mom and dad
   d. winning two million dollars

2 Who did Bobby call first?

   a. his sister
   b. his parents
   c. his wife
   d. his friend

Conversation two (Sister and Mom) 43

1 Where is Bobby going to drive?

   a. to Las Vegas
   b. to Kathmandu
   c. to L.A.
   d. to Nepal

2 How long is Bobby going to stay in Kathmandu?

   a. a few days
   b. a few weeks
   c. a few months
   d. a few years

Conversation three (Mom and Dad) 44

1 What is Bobby going to do?

   a. relax and call his parents
   b. see Mount Everest and send a postcard
   c. go hiking and swimming in the mountains
   d. send a gift and write home

2 How does Bobby's dad feel about his trip to Nepal?

   a. excited
   b. jealous
   c. angry
   d. worried

Self-study exercises

www.fifty-fifty-series.com

 **Self-study exercises**

Exercise 1 45

Listen to the conversation and check (✓) the five questions that *can* be answered. Then listen again and write the answers to the five questions.

☐ What does Brian ask Adam about?

☐ What was the weather like?

☐ What did Brian watch on TV?

☐ Where was the girl Adam met from?

☐ What was the girl's name?

☐ Where did Adam and the girl have dinner?

☐ What did Brian cook for himself?

☐ What did Brian do when he went out?

Exercise 2 46

Rewrite these sentences from the conversation in the correct order. Then listen and check your answers.

> **Memo**
> Add punctuation and use capital letters where necessary.

1 went / every day / I / skiing

_____

2 the hotel disco / I / to / went / every night

_____

3 why / me / come / Brian / didn't you / with

_____

4 vacation / OK / Brian / next / me / with / come

_____

Self-study exercise

 47

Listen to the conversation and choose the best answer to each question.

1 What is this conversation mainly about?

   a. placing a food order

   b. changing a food order

   c. canceling a food order

   d. sending back a food order

2 How does the man want his burger done?

   a. rare

   b. medium rare

   c. medium

   d. well-done

3 Who orders a baconburger?

   a. the man

   b. the woman

   c. the man and the woman

   d. no one

4 Which salad dressing does the man order?

   a. Thousand Island

   b. French

   c. Russian

   d. Italian

5 How many times does the woman change her order?

   a. once

   b. twice

   c. three times

   d. four times

6 How does the waiter act towards the man and woman?

   a. He gets annoyed.

   b. He remains professional.

   c. He becomes careless.

   d. He gets bored.

SELF-STUDY EXERCISES ANSWER KEY

UNIT 1

Exercise 1

- ☑ Dick can't do math.
- ☐
- ☑ Dad thinks the math problem is difficult.
- ☐
- ☑ Mom is good at skiing and swimming.
- ☑ Mom can speak French.
- ☑ Dad and Dick know how to play baseball.
- ☐

Exercise 2

1 You can't do math either, Dad.
2 Mom's good at a lot of things.
3 Mom knows how to play the piano.
4 You know how to cook, right?

UNIT 2

Conversation one	Conversation two	Conversation three
2	6	4
5	5	6
1	3	1
8	7	7
6	8	3
4	2	8
7	4	5
3	1	2

UNIT 3

Exercise 1

Conversation one

Woman	Excuse me, what time does the mall open?	
Man	It opens at eight ~~forty~~.	thirty
Woman	And what time does it close today?	
Man	It closes at ~~ten~~ past seven.	half

Conversation two

Woman	When do you leave for London?	
Man	I leave on February ~~nineteenth~~.	ninth
Woman	And when do you return?	
Man	I ~~return~~ on March fifteenth.	come back

Conversation three

Man	When's your ~~father's~~ birthday?	brother's
Woman	It's May twenty-third.	
Man	And when's your sister's birthday?	

Woman	Her birthday's ~~October the second~~.	the second of October

Conversation four

Man	Pardon me, when does this park open in the morning?	
Woman	It opens at a quarter ~~past~~ nine.	after
Man	And ~~when~~ does it close in the evening?	what time
Woman	It closes at half past eight.	

Exercise 2

Conversation five

Man	What day does the course begin?
Woman	It begins <u>on</u> September the sixth.
Man	When does it end?
Woman	It ends <u>on</u> the twelfth <u>of</u> December.

Conversation six

Woman	Hello? Could you tell me what time breakfast <u>is?</u>
Man	Yes, it begins <u>at</u> half past seven, in the dining room.
Woman	And what time <u>is</u> lunch?
Man	Lunch <u>starts</u> at a quarter to twelve.

Conversation seven

Man	<u>When</u> does the movie start?
Woman	It starts <u>at</u> twenty to five.
Man	Uh huh, and when does it finish?
Woman	It's <u>over</u> at ten past seven.

Conversation eight

Man	When does the beach open <u>for</u> the summer?
Woman	It opens May thirtieth.
Man	When does it close?
Woman	It closes <u>on</u> the first <u>of</u> September.

UNIT 4

Exercise 1

- ☑ Chris thinks married life is great.
- ☐
- ☑ Chris sees Mariko on weekends.
- ☑ Chris goes to work earlier.
- ☐
- ☑ Mariko does housework in the morning.
- ☐
- ☑ Chris goes to bed by eleven.

Exercise 2

1 Does she go to work in the morning?
2 So you don't have dinner together.
3 She gets home around twenty past eleven and reads until midnight.
4 So, what do you two usually do on weekends?

UNIT 6

Exercise 1

1 Pick up the magazines and put them ~~in~~ the desk.   on
2 Take the wine glasses and put them ~~under~~ the   on
   coffee table.
3 Pick up the DVD and put it ~~on~~ the TV.   under
4 Take the ~~remote control~~ and put it on the   camera
   bookcase, between the lamp and the fireplace.
5 Pick up the photo album and ~~place~~ it on the   put
   coffee table.
6 Pick up the sunglasses and put them on the ~~bed~~. desk
7 Pick up the pillow ~~on~~ the floor and put it on   from
   the sofa.
8 Take the chess set and put it ~~beside~~ the   next to
   lamp on the bookcase, on the left.

Exercise 2

1	sofa.	4	on	7	chess
2	sunglasses	5	glasses	8	photo
3	fireplace.	6	coffee		

UNIT 7

Conversation one

[T]
[F] The hotel is just around the corner.

Conversation two

[F] The man should turn right at the second corner.
[T]

Conversation three

[F] The man should turn right at the general store.
[T]

Conversation four

[F] The man is looking for the bank.
[T]

Conversation five

[T]
[F] The sheriff's office is just before the telegraph office.

UNIT 8

1	b	3	c	5	c
2	a	4	b	6	c

UNIT 9

Exercise 1

[✓] Jean's family is in the picture.
[ ]
[✓] Jean went to her uncle's house last summer.
[✓] Jean's brother is a writer.
[✓] Amy is Jean's niece.

[ ]
[✓] The name of Jean's cousin in Tina.
[ ]

Exercise 2

1 He's going to be five next month.
2 So this is your uncle, here?
3 That's his wife, Mary, on the left.
4 She painted this picture over the fireplace.

UNIT 11

Exercise 1

[✓] Ken lives in Florida.
[✓] Because it's too hot.
[ ]
[✓] Ken doesn't like fast food.
[✓] Ken thinks American football is fantastic.
[ ]
[✓] Ken likes jazz.
[ ]

Exercise 2

1 And I can't stand mosquitoes.
2 Well, I'm crazy about pizza.
3 Do you like watching TV?
4 Sometimes a little boring, but they're not bad.

UNIT 12

Conversation one	1	d	2	b
Conversation two	1	c	2	b
Conversation three	1	b	2	d

UNIT 13

Exercise 1

[✓] Brian asks Adam about his vacation.
[✓] The weather was perfect.
[ ]
[✓] The girl was from California.
[ ]
[✓] They had dinner in the hotel restaurant.
[ ]
[✓] Brian went food shopping and went to see a movie.

Exercise 2

1 I went skiing every day.
2 I went to the hotel disco every night.
3 Brian, why didn't you come with me?
4 Brian, next vacation, come with me, OK?

UNIT 14

1	a	3	c	5	c
2	d	4	c	6	b

Audio Script

Getting Started

Listening task, page 3

Exercises one and two 2–5

1	Woman	My name's Barbara. I'm from New York. I live in Canada. My hobby's photography.
2	Man	I live in Japan. My name's Alex. I'm from England. My hobby's playing tennis.
3	Woman	I'm from New Zealand. My name's Glenys. I live in Sydney. My hobby's cycling.
4	Man	I live in Colorado. My hobbies are skiing and mountain climbing. My name's Chris. I'm from Texas.

UNIT ❶

Listening task, page 6

Exercises one and two 7

Dick	I don't know how to do this!
Dad	What's that, Dick?
Dick	This math problem. I just cannot do math.
Dad	Maybe I can help you.
Dick	You can't do math either, Dad. You know that.
Dad	Let me see. Oh. That *is* difficult.
Dick	I'll ask Mom. She can do math.
Dad	Yeah, she's good at it.
Dick	Mom's good at a lot of things.
Dad	Yeah, I know, I know.
Dick	Mom knows how to play the piano—
Dad	Yeah, right. I can't do *that*, either.
Dick	… and she can play chess, and ski.
Dad	Yeah, and she can swim well.
Dick	So can I!
Dad	She knows how to speak French, too.
Dick	How about you, Dad?
Dad	Well, I can speak French a *little*, but your Mom—
Dick	No, no, I mean, what can *you* do?
Dad	Me? Well, let's see … I can swim … and I know how to play baseball. Mom doesn't know how to play baseball!
Dick	I do!
Dad	And, uh, I can … um …
Dick	You know how to cook, right?
Dad	Yeah, but Mom's better at that, too.

UNIT ❷

Listening task, page 12

Exercises one and two

Conversation one 9

Man	What do you do?
Woman	I'm a journalist.
Man	Who do you work for?
Woman	I work for *City Life Magazine*.
Man	Where do you work?
Woman	I work in London.
Man	Where are you going to stay while you're here?
Woman	With friends in New York.

Conversation two 10

Man	So tell me, Susan, what do you do?
Woman	I'm a student.
Man	Oh, really? What are you studying?
Woman	I'm studying child psychology.
Man	That's interesting. What school do you go to?
Woman	I go to UCLA. It's my first year.
Man	Oh, yeah? How do you like it?
Woman	Oh, it's great. But I'm failing French.

Conversation three 11

Man	Where are you from, Miss Ames?
Woman	I'm from Canada.
Man	Oh? Where in Canada?
Woman	Quebec.
Man	Hmm … and what do you do?
Woman	I'm a high school teacher.
Man	I see. When do you plan to return home?
Woman	Oh, in about three weeks.

UNIT ❸

Listening task, page 17

Exercises one and two

Conversation one 13

Woman	Excuse me, what time does the mall open?
Man	It opens at eight thirty.
Woman	And what time does it close today?
Man	It closes at half past seven.

Conversation two

Woman	When do you leave for London?
Man	I leave on February ninth.
Woman	And when do you return?
Man	I come back on March fifteenth.

Conversation three

Man	When's your brother's birthday?
Woman	It's May twenty-third.
Man	And when's your sister's birthday?
Woman	Her birthday's the second of October.

Conversation four

Man	Pardon me, when does this park open in the morning?
Woman	It opens at quarter after nine.
Man	And what time does it close in the evening?
Woman	It closes at half past eight.

Conversation five

Man	What day does the course begin?
Woman	It begins on September the sixth.
Man	When does it end?
Woman	It ends on the twelfth of December.

Conversation six

Woman	Hello? Could you tell me what time breakfast is?
Man	Yes, it begins at half past seven, in the dining room.
Woman	And what time is lunch?
Man	Lunch starts at a quarter to twelve.

Conversation seven

Man	When does the movie start?
Woman	It starts at twenty to five.
Man	Uh huh, and when does it finish?
Woman	It's over at ten past seven.

Conversation eight

Man	When does the beach open for the summer?
Woman	It opens May thirtieth.
Man	When does it close?
Woman	It closes on the first of September.

UNIT 4

Listening task, page 23

Exercises one, two and three

Karl	So, how do you like married life?
Chris	It's great, but I only see Mariko on weekends.
Karl	Only on weekends? Why?
Chris	Well, I go to work at a quarter after seven, and she usually gets up around nine.
Karl	Does she go to work in the morning?
Chris	No, she does housework until noon, and then drives to work after lunch, around a quarter to three.
Karl	So you don't have dinner together.
Chris	Not on weekdays. I get home at ten to six and usually eat dinner at half past seven. She gets home around twenty past eleven and reads until midnight.
Karl	What time do *you* go to bed?
Chris	I watch TV until half past ten or so, and go to bed by eleven.
Karl	So, what do you two usually do on weekends?
Chris	We talk a lot, you know, and catch up.

UNIT 5

Listening task, page 28

Exercises one and two

Conversation one

Man	Does the guard always stand inside, near the door?
Woman	Sometimes he stands outside. He usually takes a fifteen minute break around ten, and he goes out to have lunch at half past twelve.
Man	What time do they close?
Woman	Monday through Thursday they close at four, but customers usually come out until about a quarter after. Then they lock the door.
Man	I see, I see.

Conversation two

Officer	Can I see your driver's license and registration, miss?
Woman	Sure, just a moment. Uh-oh! I can't find it.
Officer	Could I have your name, please?
Woman	It's Jeanie Stone.
Officer	Is this your car, Miss Stone?

Woman	Yes, it is.
Officer	And where do you live?
Woman	I live in Levittown, at 7 Butler Lane.
Officer	Do you always drive so fast, Miss Stone?
Woman	Oh, no, I almost never speed, officer. No. Uh-uh. Not me.

Conversation three 25

Flight attendant	Pardon me, sir. Can you speak English?
Man	Yes, I can, but only a little.
Flight attendant	Are you a pilot?
Man	Excuse me?
Flight attendant	Do you know how to fly?
Man	Oh. Yes, I do. I can fly a small plane.
Flight attendant	Can you fly a large plane, like this one?
Man	I'm not sure. Why?
Flight attendant	You see, the pilot's sick and he can't land the plane.
Man	I'm sorry, could you repeat that?

Conversation four 26

Harry	Cynthia, what time is my flight? I can't find my ticket.
Cynthia	It's five thirty, Harry. Check-in is half past three. Your ticket's right there.
Harry	Oh, right. Listen, do you know the time in London now? I have to call Bob Johnson.
Cynthia	It's one fifteen in the afternoon. They usually take one hour for lunch from half past twelve in the London office.
Harry	OK, I'll call in half an hour. Do you have Bob's number? I can't find it. I can't find my glasses, either.
Cynthia	They're on your head, Harry. I'll go and get the number.

Conversation five 27

Woman	I'm here to visit my brother. He works for "Help International."
Man	And what do you do, Miss ... Miss *Jennings*, is it?
Woman	Yes, my name is Jennings and I'm a pre-school teacher.
Man	Really? Do you also work for the CIA?
Woman	What? The CIA? I don't work for the CIA! I work for "This Little Piggy Nursery School"!
Man	Why are you here?
Woman	I'm on vacation! Now I want to call my embassy! Immediately!!

UNIT 6

Listening task, page 33

Exercise one 29–36

1. Pick up the magazines and put them on the desk.
2. Take the wine glasses and put them on the coffee table.
3. Pick up the DVD and put it under the TV.
4. Take the camera and put it on the bookcase, between the lamp and the fireplace.
5. Pick up the photo album and put it on the coffee table.
6. Pick up the sunglasses and put them on the desk.
7. Pick up the pillow from the floor and put it on the sofa.
8. Take the chess set and put it next to the lamp on the bookcase, on the left.

Exercise two 37–44

1. The pillow's on the sofa.
2. The sunglasses are on the desk.
3. The camera's on the fireplace.
4. The DVD's on the TV.
5. The wine glasses are on the desk.
6. The magazines are on the coffee table.
7. The chess set's on the bookcase, next to the lamp.
8. The photo album's between the lamp and the fireplace.

UNIT 7

Listening task, page 39

Conversation one 46

Man	Pardon me, son, could you tell me where the hotel is?
Boy	Sure, mister. It's just around the corner.
Man	Left or right?
Boy	Well, turn left at the corner and it's on the right, on the corner.
Man	Thanks.

Conversation two 47

Man 1	Pardon me, do you know where the doctor's office is?
Man 2	Yeah, sure. Go straight down Main Street here and turn right at the second corner. It's on the right, in the middle of the block.
Man 1	Thank you.

Conversation three 48

Man	Excuse me ma'am. Where's the saloon?
Woman	The saloon? It's just down Main Street. Just go straight and turn right at the general store. The saloon is down Main Street, across from the hotel.
Man	Much obliged, ma'am.

Conversation four 49

Man 1	Excuse me. Could you tell me where the bank is?
Man 2	Sure. Go up Main Street for two blocks, and turn right. It's on the left, just past the feed store.

Conversation five 50

Man 1	Hey, how can I get to the sheriff's office from here?
Man 2	Turn right at the corner and it's on the left, just before the telegraph office.

UNIT 8

Listening task, page 44

Exercises one and two 52

Deb	Hello?
Pam	Hi, Sis! Did you get my letter?
Deb	Hi, Pam! Yeah, I'm looking at the photo of your classmates right now. Which one's Andrea, your roommate?
Pam	Andrea? She's wearing the white skirt and striped blouse.
Deb	Oh, yeah … she has short, curly hair? She looks nice. Is that your new boyfriend near you? The heavy-set guy with the plaid shirt?
Pam	No, Deb, that's Robert. I like *Mark*, but he's *not* my boyfriend.
Deb	OK, OK. Which one's Mark?
Pam	He's wearing a white, short-sleeved shirt.
Deb	Ohh, he's cute. Who's the short guy with the jacket and tie?
Pam	Oh, that's Albert. He's really smart, a top student … and he likes Melanie, who *never* studies. She's tall, and has long, straight hair.
Deb	*He* likes *her*?
Pam	Yeah, funny, huh?
Deb	And *who* is that girl wearing the polka dot skirt and sneakers?
Pam	That's Amy, the class clown. Her brother,

	Lee, is the heavy-set guy wearing a striped shirt. They're both really funny.
Deb	Listen, who's that tall guy with glasses, wearing the vest? He's *so* cute! Is Amy, like, his girlfriend or something?
Pam	Oh, Deb, you *are* funny! That's Rod. And he's our teacher.
Deb	He's your *teacher*?!
Pam	Just kidding.

UNIT 9

Listening task, page 50

Exercises one and two 54

Jean	Here's your coffee, Tony.
Tony	Thanks, Jean. This picture on the fireplace … is it your family?
Jean	Yeah, except for the guy with the glasses behind me. He's my uncle's friend.
Tony	Nice place.
Jean	Yeah, it's my uncle's house. I went up there with my brother's family last summer.
Tony	Your brother Paul, the writer?
Jean	Uh huh. He's next to me, holding Amy. She's my niece.
Tony	Cute kid.
Jean	Yeah, she just turned three. And her brother Bobby's in front of me.
Tony	How old's Bobby?
Jean	He's going to be five next month.
Tony	Is that your brother's wife on the right, standing next to him?
Jean	My sister-in-law? No, that's my cousin Tina. Believe it or not, she's only *sixteen*. My sister-in-law—Pamela—is next to me.
Tony	So this is your uncle, here?
Jean	Right, that's Uncle Phil.
Tony	What does he do?
Jean	He's a carpenter.
Tony	He looks young.
Jean	Oh, he's about forty-five. That's his wife, Mary, on the left. She's an artist.
Tony	An artist?
Jean	Yeah. She painted this picture over the fireplace.
Tony	This? Oh, it's, um, well, I don't know. It's, uh, very interesting, I guess. What is it?

UNIT ⑩

Listening task, page 56

Exercises one and two

Conversation one   55

Woman	Yeah, I'm on vacation, too.
Man	Do you have family in California?
Woman	Uh huh. My cousin lives in San Diego. Great place.
Man	My sister and her husband live in L.A., and I have a niece in San Bernadino, a beautiful area.
Woman	Where are you going to stay?
Man	I usually stay at my brother-in-law's house, but this time I'm staying with my niece. It's so nice there.
Woman	I always stay with my cousin. Her house is across from the beach. It's fantastic.
Man	My niece's house is in the mountains. I can't wait to land!
Woman	Yeah, California's great. Except for the earthquakes.
Man	Yeah, right, the earthquakes. And the mudslides.

Conversation two 56

Man	This is a nice place. It's huge. And expensive.
Woman	Maybe too expensive. Oh, my goodness! Is that Gary Fields?
Man	Where?
Woman	Over there. He's wearing a red tie, and he has a mustache. See him?
Man	Oh, yeah, the tall guy! Wow. Gary Fields is a *waiter*?
Woman	He was a top student in high school! And he went to a great college, didn't he? It *can't* be him.
Man	Excuse me, miss? Can you tell me that waiter's name, next to that table over there?
Waitress	His name's Gary Fields, but he's not a waiter. He's the owner.

Conversation three 57

Man	The Museum of Natural History ... Yeah, here it is. It's just across the park.
Woman	Another museum?
Man	OK, OK. You like zoos, don't you? There's a zoo right off Fifth Avenue. We go back that way and turn left. It's in Central Park.

Woman	I'm hungry, Benny.
Man	There's a cafeteria in the park.
Woman	I can't eat in a zoo—*yuck!*—I just can't.
Man	All right, all right! Oh, look. There's a pizza place across the street over there.
Woman	Where?
Man	Right there, next to the Coliseum. See it?
Woman	OK, OK. Put the map away. Let's go. I'm starving.

Conversation four 58

Brother	Hey, Sis! Where's my red sweatshirt?
Sister	I don't know. Get out of my room. Look in *your* room.
Brother	It's not in my room. Is it in your closet?
Sister	In my closet? No! Of course not.
Brother	Well, you always wear it. I never wear it. I can *never* find it! Is it under your bed?
Sister	No, it's not! Look under *your* bed.
Brother	Is that it, on your dresser?
Sister	Is that your sweatshirt? Oh. Well, hurry up and get it.
Brother	I *always* find my stuff in your room.
Sister	Yeah, yeah, yeah.
Brother	Hey, what's this in the pocket?
Sister	Give me that! Hey, come back here!

Conversation five 59

Woman	Excuse me, can you help me? I can't find Rover, he's not in his cage.
Police officer	Is he on this floor somewhere?
Woman	I don't know. Maybe he's in the basement.
Police officer	Yeah, well, maybe he's outside, on the street.
Woman	No, he always stays inside. He never goes out.
Police officer	The dog never goes out?
Woman	Rover's not a dog. He's a twelve-foot python.
Police officer	Oh, a python.
Woman	Where are you going? I told you, he's not outside!

UNIT ⑪

Listening task, page 62

Exercises one, two and three 61

Lisa	So, Ken, how do you like living in America?
Ken	I like it a lot, but I don't like the hot weather here in Florida.

125

Lisa	Yeah, it gets really hot.
Ken	And I can't stand mosquitoes.
Lisa	Yeah, right. How about American food?
Ken	Well, I'm crazy about pizza.
Lisa	Oh, yeah? How about fast food, hamburgers and stuff?
Ken	I'm sorry, but that stuff makes me sick, Lisa.
Lisa	Oh. Well, how about TV? Do you like watching TV?
Ken	Not very much. But I like watching sports. American football is fantastic!
Lisa	Really? So you watch football.
Ken	Yeah. And I watch some music channels, too.
Lisa	Oh, yeah? You like rock music?
Ken	Oh, it's OK, but I love jazz.
Lisa	Yeah, me too.
Ken	Jazz is great.
Lisa	So, what about school? How do you like your classes?
Ken	Mmm, they're OK. Sometimes a little boring, but they're not bad.

UNIT 12

Listening task, page 67

Exercises one and two

Conversation one 63

Sister	Hello?
Brother	Sis? It's me, Bobby.
Sister	Oh, hi, Bobby. Did you get back from vacation?
Brother	No, uh-uh, I'm calling from Las Vegas. I just called Mom and Dad a minute ago, but they weren't home. I have great news!
Sister	Really? What?
Brother	I won over two million dollars tonight! Can you believe it? I'm rich!
Sister	Two million dollars? Are you joking?
Brother	No, I'm not! Really! Two million, one hundred and sixty-one thousand, five hundred and twenty-five bucks!
Sister	This is unbelievable! What are you going to do?
Brother	I don't know. I think I'll buy a house in the mountains, a big house, with a fireplace in every room.
Sister	In the mountains?
Brother	Yeah! Maybe I'll go skiing every winter! But right now, I'm going to go buy a …

Conversation two 64

Sister	… and he's going to buy a new car in Las Vegas, Mom.
Mom	Las Vegas? Why in Las Vegas?
Sister	He's going to drive straight to L.A. from there, and pick up his friend, Charlie, on the way.
Mom	His friend, Charlie?
Sister	Yeah, they're going to fly to Kathmandu for a few weeks.
Mom	Kathmandu? Where's *Kathmandu*?
Sister	It's in Nepal, Mom. They're going to go there first …

Conversation three 65

Mom	… and they're going to go hiking, dear, and see Mount Everest, and, uh …
Dad	And *what*?
Mom	And, well, relax.
Dad	Why didn't he call?
Mom	He tried to call. He's going to send us a postcard, and—
Dad	A postcard?
Mom	—and maybe he'll fly home from Kathmandu.
Dad	Maybe? *Maybe*?!

UNIT 13

Listening task, page 72

Exercises one and two 67

Brian	Welcome back, Adam! How was your vacation?
Adam	It was great! I went skiing every day. The weather was perfect! How was it here?
Brian	Oh, OK, I guess. I was at home, mostly. I watched TV a lot.
Adam	Well, *I* didn't watch TV! I went to the hotel disco every night.
Brian	Yeah? How was it?
Adam	It was awesome. I met a really nice girl from California and we danced all night.
Brian	Wow!
Adam	We went ice-skating, too, and we had dinner in the hotel restaurant a few times.
Brian	Really? I cooked dinner every night.
Adam	Brian, why didn't you come with me? Why did you stay in the dormitory?
Brian	Well, I was busy. I did a lot of homework, and I read a lot of books, and … let's see—
Adam	You didn't go out at all?

Brian	Oh, sure. I went food shopping, and I even went to see a movie one evening … by myself.
Adam	Brian, next vacation, come with me, OK?
Brian	Yeah, OK, I think I will.

UNIT

Listening task, page 77

Exercises one and two

Man	Excuse me, waiter!
Waiter	Yes? Are you ready to order?
Man	Yes, we are. Susan?
Woman	I'll have a cheeseburger.
Waiter	How would you like it?
Woman	Medium, please.
Waiter	Uh huh.
Man	And I'd like a baconburger, well-done, and onion rings.
Waiter	OK.
Woman	You know what? I'll have a baconburger, too. Can you change that?
Waiter	Sure, no problem.
Woman	And could you also bring me a salad?
Man	Make that two.
Waiter	OK, and what kind of dressing would you like?
Woman	Italian, please. Wait! No, I'll have French.
Man	I'd like Russian.
Waiter	Would you care for anything to drink?
Woman	Yeah, I'd like a milk shake.
Waiter	Vanilla, chocolate or strawberry?
Woman	Vanilla.
Waiter	And you, sir?
Man	A Coke, please.
Waiter	Large or small?
Man	Large.
Woman	I'm sorry, make that chocolate.
Waiter	Sure, no problem. Anything else?
Man	No, not right now, thanks.
Waiter	Would you—
Woman	Could I also have French fries?
Waiter	Sure. French fries, OK. Would you like your drinks now?
Man	Yes, please.
Waiter	Fine. Um … miss?
Woman	Yes? Oh sure, now's fine.
Waiter	Is that … all?
Woman	Yeah. I think so.

UNIT

Listening task, page 82

Exercises one and two

Conversation one

Woman	That's right, I have two weeks. But I don't know where to go. And my vacation starts in three days!
Man	Well, do you like the beach? You can go to Hawaii. It's not too crowded this month.
Woman	I love the beach, but Hawaii is too expensive.
Man	How do you like skiing? The skiing's great in Colorado right now.
Woman	Skiing's OK, but I don't really like cold weather.
Man	Hmmm. How about Florida? It's hot, and it's not expensive.
Woman	Nah … I went there on vacation last year.
Man	Oh. Well, the Yucatan in Mexico is hot, but—
Woman	Mexico! Yes, I love Mexican food! It's fantastic! And the people are wonderful, and friendly. Yes, that's it!
Man	Great, but do you have a passport?
Woman	Oh. Do I need one?

Conversation two

Man	Where's Tracy? She was right here a minute ago.
Woman	You fell asleep, dear. Tracy went to the movies a half hour ago.
Man	Is Pat still doing her homework? I can help her now.
Woman	She finished her homework. She took her bike to the park.
Man	Oh. Well, where's Mary? She wanted me to see if—
Woman	Mary went shopping with her friends.
Man	I took a nap and everybody left?
Woman	Yes, dear. You were really out.
Man	Oh. Well, I guess it's just you and me, hon. So, what are we going to watch on TV tonight? Jane, what are we going to … Jane? Hello?

Conversation three

Man	I love Saturday morning! What are you going to do this fine morning, sweetheart?
Woman	Well, I'm going to go jogging first, and then take Poochie for a walk.
Man	Sounds great! I'm going to ride my bike over to Jay's house, and we're going to play tennis in the park.

Woman	Oh, yeah? Maybe I'll join you.
Man	Great! We can have a picnic lunch together afterwards.
Woman	Yes! I'll pack the food now, and ...
Woman	On second thought, maybe I'll do the laundry and vacuum the house.
Man	Yeah, I think I'll clean the garage and fix that doorknob.

Conversation four 73

Man	That was a good meal.
Woman	Yes, it was. The service was so-so, though.
Man	Really? I thought it was OK.
Waitress	Would you like anything else?
Man	Not me. How about you, hon?
Woman	Yes, I'd like chocolate ice cream.
Waitress	I'm sorry, but we only have vanilla, peach, strawberry and coffee ice cream.
Woman	Oh. Let me see ... OK, I'll have some apple pie.
Waitress	I'm sorry, but we have Boston cream pie, pumpkin, blueberry and banana.
Woman	I see. OK, cheesecake. Do you have cheesecake?
Waitress	I'm sorry, but we only have fruitcake—
Woman	OK, never mind.
Waitress	—chocolate layer cake, ice cream cake, assorted doughnuts, and—
Woman	Excuse me! Could we have the check, please?

Conversation five 74

Man	So, what's everyone going to have?
Woman	Franklin's going to have two hot dogs, Amanda's going to have one hot dog and one hamburger, and I'm going to have a cheeseburger. Maybe I'll have a hot dog, too.
Man	Fine. Do you like my new gas grill? I bought it yesterday. Isn't it great?
Woman	What's all that smoke?
Man	I guess the gas is a little high. Oops! Uh-oh, uh, I can't turn it down! Uh, oh no! Everything's, uh ...
Woman	Never mind, Arty, I think I'll have a salad.